Tahiti & French Polynesia Travel Guide

Unveil Hidden Gems, Cultural Treasures and Adventures with Insider Tips, Routes and Insights

Benoit Lemaigre

TABLE OF CONTENTS

CHAPTER 1: INTRODUCTION TO TAHITI & FRENCH POLYNESIA

1.1 The Allure of the Islands

The allure of Tahiti and French Polynesia is a tapestry woven from the threads of natural beauty, rich history, and vibrant culture. These islands, scattered like jewels across the South Pacific, have long captivated the imaginations of travelers, artists, and adventurers. From the moment one sets foot on these shores, the enchantment is palpable, a sensory feast that beckons exploration and discovery.

Tahiti, often referred to as the "Queen of the Pacific," serves as the gateway to French Polynesia. This island, the largest in the archipelago, is a blend of bustling urban life and serene natural landscapes. Papeete, the capital city, is a vibrant hub where the modern world meets traditional Polynesian culture. The city's markets are a riot of colors and scents, offering everything from fresh produce to intricate handicrafts. The waterfront, with its lively atmosphere and stunning views, is a perfect introduction to the island's charm.

Beyond the city, Tahiti's natural beauty unfolds in a series of breathtaking vistas. The island's interior is a lush paradise of verdant valleys, cascading waterfalls, and towering peaks. Mount Orohena, the highest point in French Polynesia, offers challenging hikes and panoramic views that reward the adventurous. The coastal areas are equally captivating, with black sand beaches on the east coast and white sand beaches on the west. The turquoise waters are a playground for snorkelers and divers, teeming with vibrant marine life and coral reefs.

The allure of Tahiti extends beyond its physical beauty. The island's history is a rich tapestry of Polynesian culture, European exploration, and colonial influence. The ancient Polynesians, master navigators and seafarers, settled these islands over a thousand years ago. Their legacy is evident in the marae, sacred stone structures that dot the landscape, and in the traditional arts of tattooing, dance, and music. The arrival of European explorers, including Captain James Cook, added new layers to the island's story, as did the subsequent French colonization.

French Polynesia, of which Tahiti is a part, comprises 118 islands and atolls spread across five archipelagos: the Society Islands, the Tuamotu Archipelago, the Marquesas Islands, the Gambier Islands, and the Austral Islands. Each group has its own unique character and attractions, contributing to the region's diverse appeal.

The Society Islands, which include Tahiti, Bora Bora, and Moorea, are perhaps the most well-known. Bora Bora, with its iconic overwater bungalows and crystal-clear lagoon, is a dream destination for honeymooners and luxury travelers. Moorea, just a short ferry ride from Tahiti, is renowned for its dramatic landscapes, with jagged peaks rising from the sea and lush valleys filled with pineapple plantations. The island's laid-back atmosphere and friendly locals make it a favorite among visitors seeking a more relaxed experience.

The Tuamotu Archipelago, a vast chain of coral atolls, offers a different kind of allure. These low-lying islands, with their pristine beaches and abundant marine life, are a paradise for divers and snorkelers. The atolls of Rangiroa and Fakarava are world-renowned for their underwater beauty, with vibrant coral gardens, schools of tropical fish, and encounters with sharks and manta rays. The Tuamotus are also a place of tranquility and solitude, where one can truly escape the hustle and bustle of modern life.

The Marquesas Islands, located to the northeast of Tahiti, are a world apart. These rugged, volcanic islands are known for their dramatic landscapes, with towering cliffs, deep valleys, and lush forests. The Marquesas have a rich cultural heritage, with ancient archaeological sites, traditional arts and crafts, and a strong sense of community. The islands' remoteness and wild beauty have inspired artists and writers, including Paul Gauguin and Herman Melville.

The Gambier Islands, a small group of volcanic islands in the southeast, are less visited but no less captivating. The islands are known for their pearl farms, producing some of the world's finest black pearls. The Gambiers also have a rich history, with ancient marae and historic churches built by early missionaries. The islands' isolation and unspoiled beauty make them a hidden gem in French Polynesia.

The Austral Islands, located to the south, are the least visited of French Polynesia's archipelagos. These islands, with their cool climate and fertile soil, are known for their agriculture, producing a variety of fruits and vegetables. The Australs are also a place of cultural richness, with traditional crafts, music, and dance. The islands' remote location and untouched landscapes offer a sense of adventure and discovery.

The allure of Tahiti and French Polynesia is not just in their physical beauty, but in the warmth and hospitality of their people. The Polynesians are known for their generosity and friendliness, welcoming visitors with open arms and sharing their rich cultural heritage. The traditional greeting, "Ia Orana," is more than just a hello; it is an invitation to experience the islands' way of life, to connect with the land and its people.

The islands' culture is a vibrant tapestry of traditions and influences. The art of tattooing, or tatau, is an ancient practice that holds deep cultural significance. Each tattoo tells a story, a personal narrative that connects the wearer to their ancestors and the land. The traditional dance, or 'ori, is a powerful expression of Polynesian identity, with its rhythmic movements and vibrant costumes. Music is an integral part of island life, from the haunting melodies of the pahu drum to the lively strumming of the ukulele.

The allure of Tahiti and French Polynesia is also in their commitment to preserving their natural and cultural heritage. Efforts to protect the islands' unique ecosystems and promote sustainable tourism are a testament to the deep connection the Polynesians have with their land and sea. Visitors are encouraged to respect the environment and support local communities, ensuring that the islands' beauty and culture can be enjoyed for generations to come.

In the end, the allure of Tahiti and French Polynesia is a multifaceted gem, a blend of natural splendor, rich history, and vibrant culture. It is a place where one can find adventure and tranquility, where the past and present coexist in harmony. Whether exploring the bustling markets of Papeete, diving in the crystal-clear waters of the Tuamotus, or hiking the rugged peaks of the Marquesas, the islands offer a journey of discovery and enchantment. The allure of Tahiti and French Polynesia is timeless, a siren call that beckons travelers to experience the magic of these islands.

1.2 Historical Background

The historical background of Tahiti and French Polynesia is a rich and complex tapestry that weaves together the stories of ancient Polynesian navigators, European explorers, and colonial powers. This intricate history has shaped the islands' culture, traditions, and identity, creating a unique blend of influences that continue to resonate today.

The origins of Polynesian settlement in Tahiti and the surrounding islands date back over a thousand years. The Polynesians, renowned for their exceptional seafaring skills, embarked on epic voyages across the vast Pacific Ocean, guided by the stars, ocean currents, and the flight patterns of birds. These early navigators settled in various island groups, including the Society Islands, where Tahiti is located. They brought with them a rich cultural heritage, including their language, social structures, and spiritual beliefs.

The ancient Polynesians established complex societies on the islands, with hierarchical systems of chiefs and priests. They built impressive structures known as marae, which served as ceremonial and religious centers. These stone platforms, often adorned with intricate carvings, were sites of worship, social gatherings, and important rituals. The marae remain significant cultural landmarks, offering a glimpse into the spiritual and social life of early Polynesian communities.

European contact with Tahiti began in the 18th century, marking a new chapter in the islands' history. The first recorded European to visit Tahiti was the British explorer Samuel Wallis, who arrived in 1767 aboard the HMS Dolphin. Wallis's encounter with the Tahitians was relatively peaceful, and he named the island "King George Island" in honor of the British monarch. However, it was the arrival of the French explorer Louis-Antoine de Bougainville in 1768 that brought Tahiti to the attention of Europe. Bougainville's romanticized accounts of the island's beauty and the hospitality of its people captured the imagination of the European public, contributing to the myth of Tahiti as a paradise on earth.

The most famous European visitor to Tahiti was Captain James Cook, who made three voyages to the island between 1769 and 1777. Cook's expeditions were significant for their scientific and navigational achievements, as well as their detailed observations of Tahitian society and culture. Cook's interactions with the Tahitians were generally amicable, and he established friendly relations with several local chiefs. His journals and the accounts of his crew provided valuable insights into the island's natural environment, social structures, and customs.

The arrival of European missionaries in the late 18th and early 19th centuries had a profound impact on Tahitian society. The London Missionary Society (LMS) sent the first group of Protestant missionaries to Tahiti in 1797. Their efforts to convert the Tahitians to Christianity were initially met with resistance, but over time, they gained influence and succeeded in establishing a foothold on the island. The missionaries introduced new religious practices, education systems, and social norms, leading to significant changes in Tahitian culture and traditions.

One of the most notable figures in this period was Pomare II, a Tahitian chief who converted to Christianity and played a key role in the spread of the new faith. Under Pomare II's leadership, the island underwent a period of transformation, with the construction of churches, schools, and the adoption of Western customs. The influence of the missionaries extended beyond religion, as they also sought to reshape Tahitian society according to their moral and ethical standards.

The 19th century saw increased European interest in Tahiti and the wider region, leading to political and territorial changes. In 1842, France established a protectorate over Tahiti and its dependencies, marking the beginning of French colonial rule. The French presence brought new administrative structures, economic policies, and cultural influences to the islands. The establishment of the French protectorate was met with resistance from some Tahitian chiefs, leading to conflicts and power struggles. However, over time, French authority was consolidated, and Tahiti became an important center of French colonial administration in the Pacific.

The colonial period brought both challenges and opportunities for the people of Tahiti and French Polynesia. The introduction of new technologies, infrastructure, and economic activities transformed the islands' way of life. The development of the copra industry, pearl farming, and other commercial enterprises provided new sources of income and employment. However, the imposition of colonial rule also led to the erosion of traditional practices, land dispossession, and social upheaval.

The 20th century was a period of significant change and modernization for Tahiti and French Polynesia. The islands played a strategic role during World War II, serving as a base for Allied forces in the Pacific theater. The post-war period saw increased efforts to develop infrastructure, education, and healthcare, as well as the growth of the tourism industry. The construction of the Faa'a International Airport in 1960 opened up the islands to international visitors, boosting the local economy and promoting cultural exchange.

The political status of French Polynesia evolved over the decades, reflecting the changing aspirations of its people. In 1957, the islands were granted the status of an Overseas Territory of France, with greater autonomy in local affairs. In 1984, French Polynesia became an Overseas Country, with further devolution of powers and the establishment of a local government. The relationship between

French Polynesia and France remains complex, with ongoing debates about autonomy, independence, and cultural identity.

The historical background of Tahiti and French Polynesia is a story of resilience, adaptation, and cultural fusion. The islands' rich heritage is celebrated through traditional arts, music, dance, and festivals, which continue to thrive alongside modern influences. The legacy of ancient Polynesian navigators, European explorers, and colonial powers is woven into the fabric of contemporary Tahitian society, creating a unique and dynamic cultural landscape.

Understanding the historical context of Tahiti and French Polynesia provides valuable insights into the islands' present-day identity and challenges. It highlights the importance of preserving cultural heritage, promoting sustainable development, and fostering a sense of community and belonging. The history of these islands is not just a record of past events, but a living narrative that continues to shape the lives and aspirations of their people.

The historical background of Tahiti and French Polynesia is a testament to the enduring spirit of its people and their ability to navigate the currents of change. It is a story of exploration, encounter, and transformation, reflecting the diverse influences that have shaped the islands over centuries. As we delve deeper into the history of Tahiti and French Polynesia, we gain a greater appreciation for the richness and complexity of this remarkable region.

1.3 Geographical Overview

Tahiti and French Polynesia, a mesmerizing archipelago in the South Pacific, offer a geographical landscape as diverse and enchanting as their cultural heritage. The region comprises 118 islands and atolls scattered over an area of more than 2,000,000 square kilometers, roughly the size of Western Europe. These islands are divided into five distinct archipelagos: the Society Islands, the Tuamotu Archipelago, the Gambier Islands, the Marquesas Islands, and the Austral Islands. Each archipelago boasts unique geographical features, ecosystems, and natural beauty, contributing to the overall allure of French Polynesia.

The Society Islands, the most well-known and visited group, include Tahiti, Moorea, Bora Bora, Huahine, Raiatea, and Taha'a. Tahiti, the largest island in French Polynesia, serves as the political and economic hub. The island is characterized by its rugged, mountainous terrain, with Mount Orohena standing as the highest peak at 2,241 meters. The lush, verdant valleys and cascading waterfalls create a dramatic landscape, while the coastal areas are fringed with black and white sand beaches. Papeete, the capital city, is located on the northwest coast of Tahiti and serves as the main gateway to the region.

Moorea, just a short ferry ride from Tahiti, is renowned for its stunning landscapes and vibrant marine life. The island's jagged peaks, such as Mount Rotui and Mount Tohivea, rise majestically from the turquoise waters of Opunohu and Cook's Bays. The coral reefs surrounding Moorea are teeming with colorful fish, making it a popular destination for snorkeling and diving enthusiasts. The island's lush interior is dotted with pineapple plantations, vanilla farms, and hiking trails that offer breathtaking views of the surrounding seascape.

Bora Bora, often referred to as the "Pearl of the Pacific," is famous for its crystal-clear lagoon and overwater bungalows. The island's central peak, Mount Otemanu, is an extinct volcano that rises 727 meters above sea level, providing a striking backdrop to the idyllic lagoon. The coral reefs encircling Bora Bora create a natural barrier, protecting the lagoon's calm, shallow waters. This unique geographical feature makes Bora Bora a haven for water sports, including snorkeling, scuba diving, and paddleboarding.

The Tuamotu Archipelago, the largest chain of atolls in the world, stretches over 1,500 kilometers and consists of 78 coral atolls. These low-lying islands are characterized by their ring-shaped coral reefs encircling shallow lagoons. The atolls of Rangiroa, Fakarava, and Tikehau are among the most famous, attracting divers from around the globe. Rangiroa, the second-largest atoll in the world, boasts a lagoon so vast it could encompass the entire island of Tahiti. The atoll's underwater world is a diver's paradise, with vibrant coral gardens, schools of tropical fish, and encounters with dolphins, sharks, and manta rays.

The Gambier Islands, located in the southeastern part of French Polynesia, are a remote and less-visited group of volcanic islands. Mangareva, the largest island, is surrounded by a lagoon and several smaller islets. The islands' volcanic origins are evident in their rugged terrain, with steep cliffs and lush vegetation. The Gambier Islands are known for their pearl farming industry, producing some of the finest black pearls in the world. The clear, nutrient-rich waters of the lagoon provide ideal conditions for cultivating these precious gems.

The Marquesas Islands, situated to the northeast of Tahiti, are among the most isolated islands in the world. This archipelago consists of 12 volcanic islands, with Nuku Hiva and Hiva Oa being the largest and most well-known. The Marquesas are characterized by their dramatic landscapes, with towering cliffs, deep valleys, and lush rainforests. The islands' rugged terrain and lack of coral reefs create a stark contrast to the other archipelagos in French Polynesia. The Marquesas are also rich in archaeological sites, with ancient stone statues, petroglyphs, and ceremonial platforms offering a glimpse into the islands' pre-European history.

The Austral Islands, located to the south of Tahiti, are a group of high volcanic islands and atolls. The main islands include Tubuai, Rurutu, Rimatara, Raivavae, and Rapa Iti. The Austral Islands are known for their cooler climate, fertile soil, and unique flora and fauna. Rurutu, for example, is famous for its limestone caves and humpback whale migrations, while Raivavae boasts pristine beaches and ancient marae. The islands' remote location and limited tourism infrastructure make them an ideal destination for travelers seeking an off-the-beaten-path experience.

The geographical diversity of French Polynesia extends beyond its islands and atolls to its marine environment. The region's coral reefs, lagoons, and open ocean waters are home to a rich array of marine life, including over 800 species of fish, 200 species of coral, and numerous species of sharks, rays, and marine mammals. The coral reefs play a crucial role in protecting the islands from storm surges and coastal erosion, while also providing habitat for marine organisms and supporting local fisheries.

The climate of French Polynesia is tropical, with two distinct seasons: the wet season (November to April) and the dry season (May to October). The wet season is characterized by higher temperatures, humidity, and frequent rainfall, while the dry season offers cooler temperatures and less precipitation. The trade winds, known as the "mara'amu," blow from the southeast and help moderate the climate, providing a refreshing breeze throughout the year.

The geographical features of French Polynesia have shaped the islands' ecosystems and biodiversity. The region's varied landscapes, from volcanic peaks to coral atolls, support a wide range of plant and animal species. The islands' flora includes tropical rainforests, coconut groves, pandanus trees, and endemic species such as the Tahitian gardenia and the Marquesan palm. The fauna of French Polynesia includes native bird species like the Tahiti monarch and the Marquesan kingfisher, as well as introduced species such as pigs, goats, and rats.

The geographical isolation of French Polynesia has also contributed to the development of unique cultural practices and traditions. The islands' natural environment has influenced the way of life of their inhabitants, from traditional fishing and agriculture to navigation and craftsmanship. The Polynesians' deep connection to the land and sea is reflected in their art, music, dance, and oral traditions, which continue to be an integral part of their cultural identity.

The geographical overview of Tahiti and French Polynesia reveals a region of stunning natural beauty and ecological diversity. The islands' varied landscapes, from towering volcanic peaks to tranquil lagoons, offer a wealth of opportunities for exploration and adventure. The rich marine environment, with its vibrant coral reefs and abundant marine life, provides a playground for water enthusiasts and nature lovers alike. The unique geographical features of French Polynesia have not only shaped its ecosystems and biodiversity but also influenced the cultural heritage and way of life of its people. This intricate interplay between geography and culture makes French Polynesia a truly captivating destination, where the natural world and human history are inextricably intertwined.

1.4 Climate and Best Times to Visit

The climate of Tahiti and French Polynesia is a quintessential tropical paradise, characterized by warm temperatures, abundant sunshine, and gentle trade winds. This idyllic weather pattern is divided into two main seasons: the wet season, which spans from November to April, and the dry season, lasting from May to October. Understanding these seasonal variations is crucial for planning a visit, as each season offers distinct experiences and opportunities.

During the wet season, the islands experience higher temperatures and increased humidity, with average daytime temperatures ranging from 25°C to 30°C (77°F to 86°F). This period is marked by frequent, though often brief, rain showers and occasional thunderstorms. The rain typically falls in the form of short, intense bursts, followed by clear skies and sunshine. The wet season also coincides with the cyclone season, although cyclones are relatively rare in French Polynesia compared to other parts of the Pacific. The lush, green landscapes and vibrant flora during this time create a picturesque setting, making it an excellent period for nature enthusiasts and photographers.

The dry season, on the other hand, is characterized by cooler temperatures, lower humidity, and minimal rainfall. Daytime temperatures during this season range from 22°C to 28°C (72°F to 82°F), providing a more comfortable climate for outdoor activities. The trade winds, known locally as the "mara'amu," blow consistently from the southeast, offering a refreshing breeze that moderates the heat. The dry season is considered the peak tourist season, as the weather conditions are ideal for beach activities, water sports, and exploring the islands' natural beauty.

For those seeking the best times to visit Tahiti and French Polynesia, the dry season from May to October is generally recommended. This period offers the most favorable weather conditions, with clear skies, calm seas, and pleasant temperatures. It is an ideal time for snorkeling, diving, and other water-based activities, as the visibility in the lagoons and reefs is at its best. The dry season coincides with several cultural events and festivals, providing visitors with an opportunity to experience the rich Polynesian heritage.

One of the most significant cultural events during the dry season is the Heiva i Tahiti, a month-long festival held in July. This celebration showcases traditional Polynesian dance, music, and sports, with participants from various islands competing in vibrant performances and competitions. The Heiva i Tahiti offers a unique insight into the local culture and traditions, making it a highlight for visitors during this time.

While the dry season is popular among tourists, the wet season also has its own charm and advantages. The increased rainfall during this period results in lush, green landscapes and blooming tropical flowers, creating a stunning backdrop for nature lovers. The wet season is also a quieter time for tourism, with fewer crowds and more opportunities for solitude and relaxation. For those interested in marine life, the wet season is an excellent time for whale watching, as humpback whales migrate to the warm waters of French Polynesia to breed and give birth between July and November.

The shoulder months of April and November offer a balance between the wet and dry seasons, with moderate temperatures and less rainfall. These months can be an ideal time to visit for those looking to avoid the peak tourist season while still enjoying favorable weather conditions. The shoulder months also provide opportunities for discounted travel and accommodation rates, making it a more budget-friendly option for travelers.

When planning a visit to Tahiti and French Polynesia, it is essential to consider the specific activities and experiences you wish to pursue. For beach lovers and water sports enthusiasts, the dry season offers the best conditions for swimming, snorkeling, and diving. The calm seas and clear waters during this period provide optimal visibility for exploring the vibrant coral reefs and marine life. The dry season is perfect for sailing, with steady trade winds creating ideal conditions for navigating the turquoise lagoons and open ocean.

For hikers and nature enthusiasts, the wet season's lush landscapes and blooming flora offer a breathtaking setting for exploring the islands' trails and natural wonders. The increased rainfall during this period results in cascading waterfalls and verdant valleys, creating a picturesque environment for outdoor adventures. However, it is essential to be prepared for occasional rain showers and muddy trails, so packing appropriate gear and clothing is advisable.

Cultural enthusiasts will find the dry season particularly appealing, as it coincides with several traditional festivals and events. The Heiva i Tahiti in July is a must-see, with its vibrant displays of Polynesian dance, music, and sports. Other cultural events, such as the Tahiti Pearl Regatta in May and the Marquesas Arts Festival in December, offer unique insights into the local heritage and traditions.

For those interested in marine life, the wet season provides excellent opportunities for whale watching and encountering other marine species. The humpback whale migration between July and November is a highlight, with these majestic creatures often seen breaching and playing in the warm waters of French Polynesia. The wet season's nutrient-rich waters attract a variety of marine life, making it a great time for diving and snorkeling.

Regardless of the season, Tahiti and French Polynesia offer a wealth of experiences and activities for visitors. The islands' diverse landscapes, from pristine beaches and turquoise lagoons to rugged mountains and lush rainforests, provide a stunning backdrop for any adventure. The warm, tropical climate ensures that visitors can enjoy outdoor activities year-round, whether it's lounging on the beach, exploring underwater worlds, or immersing themselves in the local culture.

In summary, the best time to visit Tahiti and French Polynesia depends on your preferences and interests. The dry season from May to October offers ideal weather conditions for beach activities, water sports, and cultural events, making it the peak tourist season. The wet season from November to April provides a quieter, more serene experience, with lush landscapes and excellent opportunities for whale watching and nature exploration. The shoulder months of April and November offer a balance between the two seasons, with moderate weather and fewer crowds. By considering the specific activities and experiences you wish to pursue, you can plan a visit that aligns with your interests and ensures a memorable and enjoyable trip to this tropical paradise.

1.5 Essential Travel Preparations

Traveling to Tahiti and French Polynesia requires thoughtful preparation to ensure a smooth and enjoyable experience. These islands, with their stunning landscapes and rich cultural heritage, offer a unique adventure, but being well-prepared can make all the difference.

First and foremost, it is crucial to understand the entry requirements for Tahiti and French Polynesia. As a French overseas territory, the entry regulations can vary depending on your nationality. Citizens of the European Union, the United States, Canada, Australia, and several other countries do not require a visa for stays of up to 90 days. However, a valid passport with at least six months of validity beyond your planned departure date is mandatory. It is advisable to check the latest entry requirements with the French consulate or embassy in your country before making travel arrangements, as regulations can change.

Health considerations are another important aspect of travel preparations. While Tahiti and French Polynesia are generally safe destinations, it is recommended to be up-to-date with routine vaccinations such as measles, mumps, rubella (MMR), diphtheria-tetanus-pertussis, and influenza. Vaccinations for hepatitis A and B, typhoid, and rabies may be recommended depending on your travel plans and activities. It is also wise to carry a basic first aid kit, including items such as band-aids, antiseptic wipes, pain relievers, and any prescription medications you may need. Mosquito repellent is essential, as mosquito-borne illnesses like dengue fever can occur in the region.

Travel insurance is a crucial component of your travel preparations. Comprehensive travel insurance should cover medical expenses, trip cancellations, lost luggage, and other unforeseen events. Given the remote location of some islands in French Polynesia, having coverage for medical evacuation is particularly important. Ensure that your insurance policy is valid for the entire duration of your trip and that it provides adequate coverage for the activities you plan to undertake.

When it comes to packing, the tropical climate of Tahiti and French Polynesia calls for lightweight, breathable clothing. Cotton and linen fabrics are ideal for staying cool in the warm temperatures. Swimwear is a must, as you will likely spend a significant amount of time enjoying the pristine beaches and crystal-clear waters. A wide-brimmed hat, sunglasses, and high-SPF sunscreen are essential for protecting yourself from the strong tropical sun. Comfortable walking shoes or sandals are recommended for exploring the islands, along with a pair of water shoes for navigating rocky shorelines and coral reefs.

In addition to clothing, there are several other items that can enhance your travel experience. A waterproof bag or dry sack is useful for keeping your belongings dry during water-based activities. A reusable water bottle is essential for staying hydrated, and many accommodations provide filtered water stations to refill your bottle. A lightweight rain jacket or poncho can come in handy during the wet season, as rain showers can be sudden and intense. For those planning to snorkel or dive, bringing your own mask, snorkel, and fins can ensure a comfortable fit and a more enjoyable experience.

Understanding the local currency and payment methods is also important for a hassle-free trip. The official currency of French Polynesia is the CFP franc (XPF), which is pegged to the euro. While credit and debit cards are widely accepted in hotels, restaurants, and larger shops, it is advisable to carry some cash for smaller establishments, markets, and remote areas. ATMs are available in major towns and tourist areas, but they may be scarce on smaller islands. It is a good idea to inform your bank of your travel plans to avoid any issues with card transactions.

Language can be a consideration for travelers, as French is the official language of Tahiti and French Polynesia. While many people in the tourism industry speak English, learning a few basic French phrases can enhance your interactions with locals and show respect for their culture. Simple greetings, thank you, and please can go a long way in creating positive connections.

Staying connected while traveling in French Polynesia is relatively easy, with most hotels and resorts offering Wi-Fi access. However, the quality and speed of the connection can vary, especially on more remote islands. If staying connected is important, consider purchasing a local SIM card or an international roaming plan from your mobile provider. This can provide more reliable internet access and allow you to stay in touch with family and friends.

Transportation within French Polynesia often involves inter-island flights, as the archipelago is spread over a vast area. Air Tahiti operates regular flights between the main islands, and booking in advance is recommended, especially during peak travel seasons. For shorter distances, ferries and boats are common modes of transport. Renting a car or scooter can be a convenient way to explore larger islands like Tahiti and Moorea, but be sure to familiarize yourself with local driving regulations and road conditions.

Cultural sensitivity is an important aspect of travel preparations. The people of French Polynesia are known for their warm hospitality and strong cultural traditions. Respecting local customs and etiquette can enhance your travel experience and foster positive interactions. For example, it is customary to greet people with a friendly "ia ora na" (hello) and to remove your shoes when entering someone's home. Modest dress is appreciated when visiting villages and religious sites, and it is important to seek permission before taking photographs of people or sacred places.

Finally, planning your itinerary in advance can help you make the most of your time in Tahiti and French Polynesia. Research the activities and attractions that interest you, and consider booking tours and excursions ahead of time to secure your spot. Whether you are interested in snorkeling, hiking, cultural experiences, or simply relaxing on the beach, having a well-thought-out plan can ensure a fulfilling and memorable trip.

By taking the time to prepare thoroughly, you can embark on your journey to Tahiti and French Polynesia with confidence and peace of mind. From understanding entry requirements and health considerations to packing the right essentials and respecting local customs, these preparations will help you make the most of your adventure in this tropical paradise.

CHAPTER 2: PLANNING YOUR TRIP

2.1 Choosing the Right Itinerary

Planning a trip to Tahiti and French Polynesia involves selecting an itinerary that aligns with your interests, budget, and the amount of time you have available. The archipelago, with its diverse islands and unique experiences, offers something for every type of traveler. Whether you are seeking adventure, relaxation, cultural immersion, or a mix of everything, crafting the perfect itinerary requires careful consideration.

The first step in choosing the right itinerary is to determine the duration of your trip. French Polynesia is vast, comprising 118 islands spread over five archipelagos. While it is tempting to try and see as much as possible, it is important to be realistic about the time you have. A typical vacation to French Polynesia ranges from one to two weeks, but even a shorter trip can be fulfilling if well-planned. Prioritize the islands and activities that interest you the most, and allow for some flexibility to account for travel times and unexpected delays.

Tahiti, the largest island and the gateway to French Polynesia, is often the starting point for most travelers. Papeete, the capital city, is home to the international airport and offers a range of accommodations, dining options, and cultural attractions. Spending a day or two in Tahiti allows you to acclimate to the local time zone, explore the vibrant markets, and visit historical sites such as the Museum of Tahiti and Her Islands. For nature enthusiasts, a hike to the Fautaua Waterfall or a visit to the lush Papenoo Valley provides a taste of Tahiti's natural beauty.

From Tahiti, many travelers choose to visit the nearby island of Moorea, known for its stunning landscapes and laid-back atmosphere. A short ferry ride or flight from Tahiti, Moorea offers a range of activities including snorkeling, diving, hiking, and exploring the island's picturesque villages. The island's iconic Opunohu and Cook's Bays are must-see destinations, and a visit to the Belvedere Lookout provides panoramic views of the island's lush interior. Moorea's relaxed pace makes it an ideal destination for those looking to unwind and connect with nature.

For those seeking a more luxurious and romantic experience, Bora Bora is a top choice. Often referred to as the "Pearl of the Pacific," Bora Bora is famous for its turquoise lagoon, overwater bungalows, and stunning sunsets. While Bora Bora is known for its high-end resorts, there are also more budget-friendly accommodations available. Activities on Bora Bora include snorkeling with sharks and rays, exploring the lagoon by boat, and enjoying a traditional Polynesian feast. The island's beauty and tranquility make it a popular destination for honeymooners and couples.

The Tuamotu Archipelago, known for its pristine atolls and world-class diving, is another option for travelers looking to explore beyond the main islands. Rangiroa, the largest atoll in the Tuamotus, is a diver's paradise with its crystal-clear waters and abundant marine life. The Blue Lagoon and Tiputa Pass are two of the most famous dive sites, offering encounters with dolphins, sharks, and colorful coral reefs. For those who prefer to stay above water, the atolls offer opportunities for snorkeling, kayaking, and simply relaxing on the white-sand beaches.

The Marquesas Islands, located further north, offer a more rugged and remote experience. Known for their dramatic landscapes, rich cultural heritage, and ancient archaeological sites, the Marquesas are ideal for adventurous travelers. Nuku Hiva, the largest island in the Marquesas, is home to towering cliffs, lush valleys, and traditional villages. Exploring the island's ancient tikis, petroglyphs, and ceremonial sites provides insight into the region's history and culture. The Marquesas are also a great destination for hiking, horseback riding, and experiencing traditional Polynesian life.

For a truly off-the-beaten-path experience, the Austral Islands offer a glimpse into a quieter and less-visited part of French Polynesia. The islands of Rurutu, Tubuai, and Raivavae are known for their unspoiled beauty, friendly locals, and unique cultural traditions. Rurutu, in particular, is famous for its whale-watching opportunities, as humpback whales migrate to the island's waters from July to October. The Austral Islands are perfect for travelers looking to escape the crowds and immerse themselves in the natural and cultural wonders of French Polynesia.

When planning your itinerary, it is important to consider the logistics of inter-island travel. Air Tahiti operates regular flights between the main islands, and booking flights in advance is recommended, especially during peak travel seasons. For shorter distances, ferries and boats are common modes of transport. Keep in mind that travel times can vary, and it is wise to allow for some flexibility in your schedule to account for potential delays.

Accommodations in French Polynesia range from luxury resorts and boutique hotels to guesthouses and pensions. Each type of accommodation offers a different experience, and choosing the right one depends on your preferences and budget. Luxury resorts, often located on private motus (islets), provide a high level of comfort and amenities, while guesthouses and pensions offer a more authentic and intimate experience with local hosts. Researching and booking accommodations in advance ensures that you find the best options for your needs.

Dining in French Polynesia is a delightful experience, with a mix of traditional Polynesian cuisine, French influences, and international flavors. Fresh seafood, tropical fruits, and locally grown produce are staples of the local diet. Be sure to try traditional dishes such as poisson cru (raw fish marinated in coconut milk and lime), mahi-mahi, and taro. Many islands have local markets where you can sample fresh produce and homemade treats. Dining at local restaurants and food trucks, known as roulottes, provides an opportunity to taste authentic flavors and interact with locals.

In addition to planning your itinerary, it is important to consider the best time to visit French Polynesia. The islands have a tropical climate with two main seasons: the dry season (May to October) and the wet season (November to April). The dry season is characterized by cooler temperatures, lower humidity, and less rainfall, making it the most popular time to visit. The wet season, while warmer and more humid, offers lush landscapes and fewer tourists. Whale-watching season (July to October) and the Heiva festival (July) are also popular times to visit.

Choosing the right itinerary for your trip to Tahiti and French Polynesia involves balancing your interests, budget, and the amount of time you have available. Whether you are drawn to the luxury of Bora Bora, the adventure of the Marquesas, or the tranquility of the Austral Islands, careful planning ensures a memorable and fulfilling experience. By considering the logistics of inter-island travel, selecting the right accommodations, and timing your visit to coincide with your preferred activities, you can create an itinerary that captures the essence of this tropical paradise.

2.2 Budgeting for Your Adventure

Budgeting for a trip to Tahiti and French Polynesia requires careful planning and consideration of various factors to ensure a memorable and stress-free experience. The islands, known for their stunning beauty and unique culture, can be an expensive destination, but with the right strategies, it is possible to enjoy this tropical paradise without breaking the bank.

The first step in budgeting for your adventure is to determine the overall amount you are willing to spend. This includes not only the major expenses such as flights and accommodations but also daily costs like meals, activities, and transportation. Setting a realistic budget helps you make informed decisions and prioritize your spending.

Flights to French Polynesia are often one of the largest expenses. Booking your flights well in advance can result in significant savings. Keep an eye out for deals and discounts offered by airlines, and consider flying during the off-peak season when prices are generally lower. Being flexible with your travel dates and routes can help you find more affordable options. For example, flying into Tahiti from major hubs like Los Angeles or Auckland may offer better rates compared to other departure cities.

Accommodations in French Polynesia range from luxury resorts to budget-friendly guesthouses. While overwater bungalows are a dream for many travelers, they come with a hefty price tag. To save on accommodations, consider staying in pensions or guesthouses, which offer a more authentic and intimate experience. These family-run establishments often provide comfortable lodging at a fraction of the cost of high-end resorts. Another option is to split your stay between different types of accommodations, allowing you to experience both luxury and budget-friendly options.

Dining in French Polynesia can also be a significant expense, especially if you choose to eat at high-end restaurants. To manage your food budget, explore local markets and food trucks, known as roulottes, which offer delicious and affordable meals. Sampling fresh produce, seafood, and traditional Polynesian dishes from these vendors not only saves money but also provides an opportunity to experience the local cuisine. Many guesthouses and pensions include breakfast in their rates, which can further reduce your daily food costs.

Transportation between the islands is another important consideration. Air Tahiti operates flights to many of the islands, and purchasing an island-hopping pass can be a cost-effective way to explore multiple destinations. These passes offer a set number of flights within a specific time frame, allowing you to visit several islands without the need to book individual tickets. For shorter distances, ferries and boats are a more budget-friendly option. Renting a car or scooter on the larger islands can also be a convenient and economical way to get around.

Activities and excursions are a highlight of any trip to French Polynesia, but they can quickly add up. Prioritize the experiences that are most important to you and look for ways to save on others. Many islands offer free or low-cost activities such as hiking, snorkeling, and exploring local villages. Renting equipment for water sports like kayaking or paddleboarding can be more affordable than booking guided tours. Some guesthouses and pensions provide complimentary or discounted activities for their guests.

Travel insurance is an essential part of your budget, providing peace of mind in case of unexpected events such as medical emergencies, trip cancellations, or lost luggage. While it may seem like an additional expense, the protection it offers can save you from significant financial losses. Shop around for travel insurance policies that offer comprehensive coverage at a reasonable price.

Currency exchange rates and transaction fees can also impact your budget. French Polynesia uses the CFP franc (XPF), and it is advisable to exchange some currency before you arrive or withdraw cash from ATMs on the islands. Be aware of any fees associated with using your credit or debit cards abroad, and consider using a travel card that offers favorable exchange rates and low or no foreign transaction fees.

Souvenirs and gifts are another aspect to consider in your budget. While it is tempting to buy numerous mementos, focus on meaningful and locally made items that support the local economy. Traditional Polynesian crafts, such as hand-carved tikis, pareos (sarongs), and black pearl jewelry, make unique and memorable souvenirs. Shopping at local markets and directly from artisans can also result in better prices and a more authentic experience.

To make the most of your budget, it is helpful to track your expenses throughout your trip. Keeping a daily record of your spending allows you to stay within your budget and make adjustments as needed. There are various apps and tools available that can help you monitor your expenses and manage your finances while traveling.

Another way to save money is to travel with a group or join a tour. Group travel often comes with discounts on accommodations, activities, and transportation. Sharing costs with travel companions can make certain expenses more manageable. If you prefer independent travel, consider joining day tours or excursions that offer group rates.

Lastly, it is important to be mindful of hidden costs that can arise during your trip. These may include resort fees, tips, and charges for additional services such as Wi-Fi or laundry. Being aware of these potential expenses and factoring them into your budget helps avoid any surprises and ensures a smoother travel experience.

Budgeting for a trip to Tahiti and French Polynesia involves careful planning and consideration of various factors. By setting a realistic budget, prioritizing your spending, and exploring cost-saving options, you can enjoy the beauty and culture of this tropical paradise without overspending. Whether you are staying in luxury resorts or budget-friendly guesthouses, dining at high-end restaurants or local food trucks, the key is to find a balance that allows you to experience the best of French Polynesia while staying within your means.

2.3 Travel Insurance and Safety Tips

Travel insurance and safety are crucial aspects of planning any trip, especially to a destination as remote and unique as Tahiti and French Polynesia. These islands, while breathtakingly beautiful, present their own set of challenges and risks that travelers must be prepared for. Ensuring you have the right travel insurance and understanding the safety tips specific to this region can make your adventure both enjoyable and secure.

Travel insurance is an essential investment for any trip, providing coverage for unexpected events that could otherwise result in significant financial losses. When selecting a travel insurance policy for your trip to Tahiti and French Polynesia, consider the following key components: medical coverage, trip cancellation and interruption, baggage loss and delay, and emergency evacuation.

Medical coverage is perhaps the most critical aspect of travel insurance. While Tahiti and the larger islands have medical facilities, the more remote islands may have limited healthcare services. A comprehensive travel insurance policy should cover medical expenses, including hospital stays, doctor visits, and prescription medications. Additionally, ensure that your policy includes coverage for medical evacuation, which can be extremely costly if you need to be transported to a facility with more advanced medical care.

Trip cancellation and interruption coverage protect you financially if you need to cancel or cut short your trip due to unforeseen circumstances such as illness, natural disasters, or other emergencies. This coverage typically reimburses you for non-refundable expenses such as flights, accommodations, and tours.

Given the high cost of travel to French Polynesia, this type of coverage can provide significant peace of mind.

Baggage loss and delay coverage is another important component of travel insurance. Losing your luggage or experiencing delays can be particularly challenging in a remote destination where replacing essential items may be difficult and expensive. This coverage reimburses you for the cost of replacing lost or delayed items, ensuring you can continue your trip with minimal disruption.

Emergency evacuation coverage is crucial for travelers visiting remote or less accessible areas of French Polynesia. In the event of a natural disaster, political unrest, or medical emergency, this coverage ensures you can be safely evacuated to a secure location or medical facility. Given the geographical isolation of many islands, having this coverage can be a lifesaver.

When purchasing travel insurance, it is essential to read the policy details carefully and understand what is covered and what is not. Pay attention to any exclusions or limitations, such as pre-existing medical conditions or high-risk activities like scuba diving or hiking. If you plan to engage in adventure sports, ensure your policy includes coverage for these activities.

In addition to travel insurance, being aware of safety tips specific to Tahiti and French Polynesia can help you avoid potential risks and enjoy a worry-free trip. One of the primary concerns for travelers in this region is the natural environment. The islands are prone to natural disasters such as cyclones, earthquakes, and tsunamis. Familiarize yourself with the local emergency procedures and evacuation routes, and stay informed about weather conditions and potential hazards during your stay.

The tropical climate of French Polynesia also presents health risks such as sunburn, dehydration, and mosquito-borne illnesses like dengue fever and Zika virus. Protect yourself from the sun by wearing sunscreen, hats, and lightweight, long-sleeved clothing. Stay hydrated by drinking plenty of water, especially during outdoor activities. To prevent mosquito bites, use insect repellent, sleep under mosquito nets, and stay in accommodations with screened windows and doors.

Water safety is another important consideration. While the crystal-clear waters of French Polynesia are inviting, they can also be dangerous. Strong currents, sharp coral, and marine life such as jellyfish and sea urchins pose risks to swimmers and snorkelers. Always swim in designated areas, follow local safety guidelines, and wear appropriate footwear to protect your feet from sharp objects.

When exploring the islands, be mindful of your surroundings and take precautions to protect your belongings. Petty crime, such as theft and pickpocketing, can occur in tourist areas. Keep your valuables secure, avoid displaying expensive items, and use hotel safes to store passports, money, and other important documents. When using public transportation or walking in crowded areas, remain vigilant and be aware of your surroundings.

Respecting the local culture and customs is also essential for a safe and enjoyable trip. The people of French Polynesia are known for their warm hospitality, but it is important to be mindful of cultural norms and practices. Dress modestly when visiting villages and religious sites, and always ask for permission before taking photographs of people or their property. Learning a few basic phrases in French or Tahitian can go a long way in building rapport with locals and showing respect for their culture.

If you plan to rent a car or scooter, familiarize yourself with the local traffic laws and road conditions. Driving in French Polynesia can be challenging due to narrow roads, sharp curves, and occasional livestock on the road. Always wear a helmet when riding a scooter, and exercise caution when driving, especially at night or in unfamiliar areas.

For those planning to engage in water sports or adventure activities, ensure you use reputable operators who prioritize safety. Check that equipment is in good condition and that guides are experienced and certified. Follow all safety instructions and guidelines provided by the operators, and do not take unnecessary risks.

Finally, it is important to have a plan in case of emergencies. Keep a list of emergency contacts, including local authorities, your country's embassy or consulate, and your travel insurance provider. Know the location of the nearest medical facilities and have a basic first aid kit on hand. In the event of an emergency, remain calm and follow the instructions of local authorities and emergency personnel.

By investing in comprehensive travel insurance and following these safety tips, you can ensure a secure and enjoyable trip to Tahiti and French Polynesia. Being prepared for potential risks and taking proactive measures to protect yourself and your belongings allows you to fully immerse yourself in the beauty and culture of this tropical paradise. Whether you are exploring the vibrant coral reefs, hiking through lush rainforests, or relaxing on pristine beaches, peace of mind is an invaluable companion on your journey.

2.4 Packing Essentials

Packing for a trip to Tahiti and French Polynesia requires careful consideration to ensure you have everything you need for a comfortable and enjoyable experience. The tropical climate, diverse activities, and remote locations mean that packing the right essentials can make a significant difference in your travel experience. Here's a comprehensive guide to help you prepare for your adventure.

Clothing is one of the most important aspects to consider when packing for Tahiti and French Polynesia. The weather is typically warm and humid, so lightweight, breathable fabrics are essential. Pack plenty of shorts, t-shirts, tank tops, and sundresses made from materials like cotton or linen. These fabrics will keep you cool and comfortable in the tropical heat. Additionally, bring a few long-sleeved shirts and lightweight pants for protection against mosquitoes in the evenings.

Swimwear is a must for any trip to French Polynesia. Pack at least two or three swimsuits so you always have a dry one available. Consider bringing a rash guard or swim shirt for added sun protection during water activities like snorkeling or paddleboarding. A sarong or cover-up is also useful for transitioning from the beach to other activities.

Footwear should be practical and comfortable. Flip-flops or sandals are ideal for the beach and casual outings, while a pair of sturdy water shoes will protect your feet from sharp coral and rocks when exploring the lagoons. If you plan to hike or explore the islands' interior, bring a pair of comfortable walking shoes or hiking sandals with good grip.

Sun protection is crucial in the tropical sun of French Polynesia. Pack a wide-brimmed hat to shield your face and neck from the sun's rays, along with a pair of UV-protective sunglasses. High-SPF sunscreen is essential, and it's a good idea to bring more than you think you'll need, as it can be expensive to purchase locally. Look for reef-safe sunscreen to protect the delicate marine ecosystems. Lip balm with SPF protection is also important to prevent sunburned lips.

Insect repellent is another essential item, as mosquitoes can be prevalent, especially in the evenings. Choose a repellent that contains DEET or another effective ingredient, and consider bringing a mosquito net if you plan to stay in more rustic accommodations. Anti-itch cream or hydrocortisone can be helpful for treating any bites you do get.

A basic first aid kit is always a good idea when traveling, especially to remote destinations. Include items like adhesive bandages, antiseptic wipes, pain relievers, and any prescription medications you may need. Motion sickness medication can be useful if you plan to take boat trips between the islands. Additionally, pack any personal hygiene items you may need, such as toothbrush and toothpaste, deodorant, and feminine hygiene products.

Electronics and accessories can enhance your travel experience. A waterproof camera or a GoPro is perfect for capturing underwater adventures and stunning landscapes. Don't forget extra memory cards and batteries or a portable charger to keep your devices powered up. A universal power adapter is essential for charging your electronics, as the outlets in French Polynesia may differ from those in your home country.

Travel documents and money should be organized and easily accessible. Bring your passport, along with copies of important documents like your travel insurance policy, flight itinerary, and accommodation reservations. It's also a good idea to have some local currency (CFP Franc) on hand for small purchases, as not all places accept credit cards. A money belt or hidden pouch can help keep your valuables secure.

Entertainment and reading materials can make long flights and downtime more enjoyable. Pack a good book, e-reader, or download some movies and music to your devices. A travel journal is also a great way to document your experiences and memories.

Reusable items can help reduce your environmental impact while traveling. Bring a reusable water bottle to stay hydrated and reduce plastic waste. A reusable shopping bag is handy for carrying souvenirs or groceries. If you plan to snorkel frequently, consider bringing your own snorkel gear to avoid using rental equipment.

When packing, it's important to consider the specific activities you plan to do. If you're an avid snorkeler or diver, bring your own mask, snorkel, and fins for a more comfortable fit. For those interested in hiking, pack a lightweight backpack, a reusable water bottle, and a small first aid kit. If you plan to visit cultural sites or attend traditional ceremonies, bring modest clothing that covers your shoulders and knees as a sign of respect.

Packing cubes or compression bags can help you organize your belongings and save space in your luggage. Use them to separate different types of clothing and keep your suitcase neat and tidy. A lightweight, foldable daypack is also useful for carrying essentials during day trips and excursions.

Finally, consider the luggage itself. A durable, lightweight suitcase or backpack is ideal for navigating airports and ferry terminals. If you plan to visit multiple islands, a backpack may be more convenient for carrying your belongings. Make sure your luggage is easily identifiable with a luggage tag or a unique marker to avoid confusion at baggage claim.

By carefully considering your packing essentials and tailoring them to the unique environment and activities of Tahiti and French Polynesia, you can ensure a smooth and enjoyable trip. Proper preparation allows you to focus on the incredible experiences and natural beauty that await you in this tropical paradise. Whether you're lounging on pristine beaches, exploring vibrant coral reefs, or immersing yourself in the rich Polynesian culture, having the right gear and essentials will enhance your adventure and create lasting memories.

2.5 Navigating Local Transportation

Navigating local transportation in Tahiti and French Polynesia can be an adventure in itself, offering a unique glimpse into the daily life and culture of these stunning islands. Understanding the various modes of transport available will help you move around efficiently and make the most of your trip.

The primary gateway to French Polynesia is Faa'a International Airport in Papeete, Tahiti. From here, you can access the other islands via domestic flights, ferries, and boats. Air Tahiti is the main domestic airline, offering flights to most of the inhabited islands. Booking flights in advance is advisable, especially during peak travel seasons, to secure the best rates and availability. The airline operates on a hub-and-spoke system, with Papeete as the central hub, so you may need to return to Tahiti to connect to other islands.

Ferries and boats are popular options for inter-island travel, providing a scenic and often more affordable alternative to flying. The Aremiti and Terevau ferries operate regular services between Tahiti and Moorea, a journey that takes about 30-45 minutes. For longer routes, such as those to the Tuamotu or Marquesas archipelagos, cargo-passenger ships like the Aranui 5 offer a unique travel experience, combining transportation with a cruise-like atmosphere. These voyages can take several days, providing ample opportunity to explore remote islands and interact with locals.

Once you arrive on an island, getting around can vary depending on its size and infrastructure. On larger islands like Tahiti and Moorea, rental cars are a convenient option, giving you the freedom to explore at your own pace. Several international and local car rental agencies operate in Papeete and at major hotels. Be sure to have a valid driver's license and familiarize yourself with local driving laws and customs. Traffic drives on the right side of the road, and while the main roads are generally well-maintained, some rural areas may have rougher terrain.

For those who prefer not to drive, taxis and private transfers are readily available in more populated areas. Taxis can be found at airports, ferry terminals, and major hotels. It's a good idea to agree on a fare before starting your journey, as taxis in French Polynesia do not always use meters. Private transfers can be arranged through your accommodation or travel agent, offering a more personalized and often more comfortable option.

Public transportation is limited but can be an interesting way to experience local life. In Tahiti, the public bus system, known as Le Truck, used to be a popular mode of transport, but it has been largely replaced by modern buses. These buses operate on fixed routes around the island, with schedules that can be somewhat irregular. They are an affordable option for getting around, especially for short distances. On some of the smaller islands, public transportation may be non-existent, and walking or biking can be the best way to explore.

Bicycles and scooters are popular on many islands, offering a fun and eco-friendly way to get around. Rentals are available at most hotels and guesthouses, and some islands have dedicated bike paths. Scooters are a great option for covering longer distances or exploring more remote areas, but be sure to wear a helmet and exercise caution, especially on unfamiliar roads.

For water-based transportation, outrigger canoes, kayaks, and paddleboards are widely available for rent. These traditional Polynesian vessels offer a unique way to explore the lagoons and coastline, providing a closer connection to the natural beauty of the islands. Guided tours are also available, offering insights into the local marine life and ecosystems.

When planning your transportation, it's important to consider the logistics of island hopping. Some islands are more remote and less frequently serviced by flights or ferries, so careful planning is essential to ensure you can reach your desired destinations. Allow extra time for connections and be prepared for potential delays, as weather conditions can sometimes affect travel schedules.

In addition to the practical aspects of transportation, it's worth considering the cultural experience of traveling in French Polynesia. The pace of life is generally slower and more relaxed, and this is reflected in the transportation options. Embrace the opportunity to interact with locals, whether it's chatting with your taxi driver, sharing a ferry ride with island residents, or joining a guided tour. These interactions can provide valuable insights into the local way of life and enhance your overall travel experience.

For those seeking a more luxurious travel experience, private yacht charters are available, offering the ultimate in comfort and flexibility. These charters can be tailored to your preferences, allowing you to explore the islands at your own pace and access more secluded areas. While this option can be more expensive, it provides a unique and memorable way to experience the beauty of French Polynesia.

In summary, navigating local transportation in Tahiti and French Polynesia requires a mix of planning and flexibility. By understanding the various options available and considering your own preferences and travel style, you can create a seamless and enjoyable travel experience. Whether you're flying between islands, cruising on a ferry, or exploring by bike or kayak, the journey itself can be a highlight of your trip, offering new perspectives and unforgettable memories.

CHAPTER 3: MUST-SEE DESTINATIONS

3.1 Tahiti: The Heart of French Polynesia

Tahiti, often referred to as the heart of French Polynesia, is a vibrant island that serves as the main gateway to this enchanting archipelago. With its lush landscapes, rich cultural heritage, and bustling capital city, Tahiti offers a diverse array of experiences for travelers. The island is divided into two parts: Tahiti Nui, the larger, more populated section, and Tahiti Iti, the smaller, more remote peninsula. Each area has its own unique charm and attractions, making Tahiti a must-see destination for any visitor to French Polynesia.

Papeete, the capital city, is the bustling epicenter of Tahiti Nui. This lively city is a blend of modernity and tradition, offering a glimpse into the daily life of Tahitians. The Papeete Market, or Marché de Papeete, is a vibrant hub where locals and tourists alike can explore a variety of goods, from fresh produce and seafood to handmade crafts and souvenirs. The market is an excellent place to immerse yourself in the local culture, sample traditional Polynesian foods, and purchase unique gifts to take home.

A short walk from the market, the waterfront promenade, known as Le Quai des Ferries, offers stunning views of the harbor and is a popular spot for leisurely strolls. Here, you can watch the ferries come and go, enjoy a meal at one of the many waterfront restaurants, or simply relax and take in the scenery. The nearby Place Vai'ete is another lively area, especially in the evenings when food trucks, known as roulottes, set up shop, offering a variety of delicious and affordable meals.

For those interested in history and culture, the Museum of Tahiti and Her Islands provides a comprehensive overview of the region's rich heritage. The museum's exhibits cover everything from ancient Polynesian artifacts to the impact of European colonization. It's an educational experience that offers valuable insights into the island's past and its enduring traditions.

Nature enthusiasts will find plenty to explore in Tahiti's lush interior. The island is home to several stunning waterfalls, including the Faarumai Waterfalls, located in the northeastern part of Tahiti Nui. These three cascading falls are surrounded by verdant vegetation and offer a serene escape from the hustle and bustle of Papeete. Another natural wonder is the Arahoho Blowhole, a geological formation where waves crash into a lava tube, creating dramatic spouts of water.

Tahiti Iti, the smaller peninsula, offers a more tranquil and remote experience. This area is less developed and provides a glimpse into the traditional Polynesian way of life. The village of Teahupo'o, located on the southwestern coast of Tahiti Iti, is world-renowned for its powerful surf break. Surfers from around the globe flock to Teahupo'o to ride its legendary waves, but even if you're not a surfer, the village is worth a visit for its stunning coastal scenery and laid-back atmosphere.

For a truly immersive experience, consider taking a guided hike into the Fenua 'Aihere, a remote and pristine area of Tahiti Iti. This region is accessible only by foot or boat and offers a unique opportunity to explore untouched rainforests, hidden waterfalls, and ancient archaeological sites. Local guides can provide valuable insights into the flora, fauna, and history of the area, making it a memorable adventure.

No visit to Tahiti would be complete without experiencing its beautiful beaches. While the island is not as famous for its beaches as some of its neighbors, it still boasts several stunning spots to relax and soak up the sun. La Plage de Maui, located on the southern coast of Tahiti Nui, is one of the island's most popular beaches. Its white sand and crystal-clear waters make it an ideal spot for swimming, snorkeling, and picnicking. Another notable beach is Pointe Venus, located on the northern coast. This black sand beach is steeped in history, as it was the landing site of several famous explorers, including Captain James Cook.

For those seeking adventure, Tahiti offers a variety of water-based activities. The island's lagoons and reefs are perfect for snorkeling and diving, with an abundance of marine life to discover. Several dive operators offer excursions to popular sites, such as the Aquarium, a shallow dive spot teeming with colorful fish and coral. For a more unique experience, consider a night dive to witness the bioluminescent plankton that light up the underwater world.

Sailing and boating are also popular activities in Tahiti. Renting a boat or joining a sailing tour allows you to explore the island's coastline and nearby islets at your own pace. The calm waters of the lagoon are perfect for kayaking and paddleboarding, providing a peaceful way to take in the natural beauty of the island.

Tahiti's vibrant culture is celebrated through various festivals and events held throughout the year. One of the most significant is Heiva i Tahiti, a month-long celebration of Polynesian culture that takes place in July. The festival features traditional dance performances, music, sports competitions, and craft exhibitions, offering a deep dive into the island's cultural heritage. Another notable event is the Tahiti Pearl Regatta, an annual sailing race that attracts participants from around the world and showcases the island's maritime traditions.

Culinary enthusiasts will find plenty to savor in Tahiti. The island's cuisine is a fusion of Polynesian, French, and Asian influences, resulting in a diverse and flavorful dining scene. Traditional dishes, such as poisson cru (raw fish marinated in coconut milk and lime juice) and ma'a tinito (a hearty stew of pork, beans, and vegetables), are must-tries. For a more upscale dining experience, several restaurants in Papeete offer gourmet meals featuring fresh, locally-sourced ingredients.

Accommodations in Tahiti range from luxury resorts to budget-friendly guesthouses, catering to a variety of travel styles and budgets. Many of the island's resorts are located along the west coast, offering stunning sunset views and easy access to the lagoon. For a more authentic experience, consider staying in a family-run pension or guesthouse, where you can enjoy warm hospitality and gain insights into the local way of life.

Tahiti, with its blend of natural beauty, rich culture, and modern amenities, truly embodies the spirit of French Polynesia. Whether you're exploring the bustling streets of Papeete, hiking through lush rainforests, or relaxing on a pristine beach, the island offers a diverse array of experiences that will leave a lasting impression.

3.2 Bora Bora: The Romantic Paradise

Bora Bora, often hailed as the jewel of the South Pacific, is a destination that epitomizes romance and luxury. This small island, surrounded by a stunning turquoise lagoon and a barrier reef, offers an idyllic setting for honeymooners, couples, and anyone seeking a slice of paradise. The island's dramatic landscape, dominated by the iconic Mount Otemanu, provides a breathtaking backdrop for a myriad of activities and experiences.

Upon arrival, the first thing that strikes visitors is the sheer beauty of Bora Bora's lagoon. The crystal-clear waters, teeming with vibrant marine life, are perfect for snorkeling and diving. Coral gardens, such as the Coral Gardens near the Sofitel Bora Bora Private Island, offer an underwater spectacle of colorful corals and tropical fish. For those new to snorkeling, guided tours provide equipment and expert advice, ensuring a safe and enjoyable experience.

One of the most popular activities in Bora Bora is a lagoon tour. These excursions often include stops at various snorkeling spots, a visit to a stingray and shark feeding area, and a traditional Polynesian picnic on a motu (small islet). The experience of swimming alongside graceful stingrays and blacktip reef sharks is both exhilarating and unforgettable. The picnic, typically featuring local dishes such as poisson cru and grilled fish, allows visitors to savor the flavors of Polynesia while enjoying the serene beauty of a secluded beach.

For a more intimate exploration of the lagoon, consider renting a kayak or paddleboard. Paddling through the calm waters at your own pace offers a sense of tranquility and allows for close encounters with the lagoon's diverse marine life. Many resorts provide complimentary equipment, making it easy to embark on a solo adventure.

Bora Bora's overwater bungalows are synonymous with luxury and romance. These iconic accommodations, perched above the lagoon on stilts, offer unparalleled views and direct access to the water. Waking up to the sight of the sun rising over Mount Otemanu, with the gentle sound of the lagoon lapping beneath you, is an experience that epitomizes the allure of Bora Bora. Many bungalows feature glass floor panels, allowing guests to observe the marine life below without leaving the comfort of their room.

While the overwater bungalows are a highlight, Bora Bora also offers a range of accommodations to suit different budgets and preferences. From luxurious resorts with private villas to charming guesthouses that provide a more authentic Polynesian experience, there is something for everyone. Staying in a family-run pension, for example, offers the opportunity to connect with locals and gain insights into their way of life.

Exploring the island itself reveals a wealth of natural beauty and cultural heritage. A 4x4 safari tour is an excellent way to discover Bora Bora's interior, including its lush valleys, ancient marae (sacred sites), and World War II relics. These tours often include stops at panoramic viewpoints, such as the lookout at Matira Point, which offers stunning vistas of the lagoon and surrounding motus. Knowledgeable guides share stories and legends, providing a deeper understanding of the island's history and culture.

For those who prefer a more active exploration, hiking trails lead to some of Bora Bora's most scenic spots. The hike to the summit of Mount Pahia, while challenging, rewards adventurers with breathtaking views of the island and lagoon. Another popular trail is the hike to the Valley of the Kings, which passes through lush vegetation and ancient archaeological sites.

Bora Bora's culinary scene is a delightful fusion of Polynesian, French, and international flavors. Dining at one of the island's gourmet restaurants, such as La Villa Mahana, offers a memorable experience with dishes crafted from fresh, locally-sourced ingredients. For a more casual meal, the island's food trucks, known as roulottes, serve up delicious and affordable options, from fresh seafood to crepes.

A romantic dinner on the beach, with the sound of the waves and the stars overhead, is a quintessential Bora Bora experience. Many resorts offer private dining experiences, where guests can enjoy a gourmet meal in a secluded setting. Whether it's a candlelit dinner on the sand or a picnic on a private motu, these intimate moments create lasting memories.

Bora Bora's vibrant culture is celebrated through various events and festivals. The Heiva i Bora Bora, held in July, is a highlight, featuring traditional dance performances, music, and sports competitions. This month-long celebration offers a deep dive into Polynesian culture and traditions, with locals and visitors coming together to enjoy the festivities.

For those seeking relaxation and rejuvenation, Bora Bora's spas offer a range of treatments inspired by Polynesian traditions. A massage using monoi oil, a fragrant blend of coconut oil and tiare flowers, is a soothing way to unwind. Many spas are located in stunning settings, such as overwater bungalows or beachfront pavilions, enhancing the sense of tranquility.

Shopping in Bora Bora provides the opportunity to purchase unique souvenirs and local crafts. The island's boutiques and markets offer a variety of items, from black pearls and handwoven hats to pareos (sarongs) and wood carvings. Black pearls, in particular, are a sought-after memento, with several reputable jewelers offering exquisite pieces.

Bora Bora's nightlife, while more subdued than some other destinations, offers a range of options for evening entertainment. Many resorts feature live music and traditional dance shows, providing a taste of Polynesian culture. For a more laid-back evening, enjoying a cocktail at a beachfront bar while watching the sunset is a perfect way to end the day.

The island's warm and welcoming people are an integral part of the Bora Bora experience. The genuine hospitality and friendliness of the locals create a sense of connection and make visitors feel at home. Engaging with the community, whether through a cultural tour or simply chatting with locals, enriches the travel experience and provides a deeper appreciation of the island's way of life.

Bora Bora, with its stunning natural beauty, luxurious accommodations, and rich cultural heritage, offers a romantic paradise that captivates the heart and soul. Whether you're exploring the vibrant marine life of the lagoon, savoring a gourmet meal under the stars, or simply relaxing on a pristine beach, the island provides a myriad of experiences that create lasting memories.

3.3 Moorea: The Magical Island

Moorea, often referred to as the "Magical Island," is a gem in the heart of French Polynesia. Just a short ferry ride from Tahiti, Moorea captivates visitors with its lush landscapes, crystal-clear waters, and vibrant culture. The island's dramatic volcanic peaks, verdant valleys, and pristine beaches create a picturesque setting that feels like a dream come true.

The first glimpse of Moorea from the ferry is nothing short of breathtaking. The island's jagged peaks, including the iconic Mount Rotui and Mount Tohivea, rise majestically from the sea, creating a stunning silhouette against the sky. As the ferry approaches the island, the turquoise waters of the lagoon come into view, inviting travelers to dive into the adventure that awaits.

One of the best ways to explore Moorea is by renting a car or scooter. The island's well-maintained roads make it easy to navigate, and a self-guided tour allows for the flexibility to stop and explore at your own pace. The coastal road, which circles the island, offers spectacular views and access to many of Moorea's top attractions.

A visit to the Belvedere Lookout is a must for any traveler to Moorea. This vantage point, located in the island's interior, provides panoramic views of Cook's Bay and Opunohu Bay, as well as the surrounding mountains and valleys. The drive to the lookout takes you through lush pineapple plantations and dense tropical forests, offering a glimpse of the island's agricultural heritage.

For those who enjoy hiking, Moorea offers several trails that showcase the island's natural beauty. The Three Coconuts Pass hike is a popular choice, leading adventurers through dense jungle and up to a saddle between two peaks. The trail offers stunning views of the island's interior and the surrounding ocean, making the effort well worth it. Another rewarding hike is the trek to the Afareaitu Waterfall, where a refreshing dip in the cool waters provides a perfect respite from the tropical heat.

Moorea's lagoon is a playground for water enthusiasts. Snorkeling and diving are top activities, with the island's coral reefs teeming with marine life. The Lagoonarium, an open-water aquarium, offers a unique opportunity to swim with rays, sharks, and a variety of colorful fish in a controlled environment. For a more immersive experience, guided snorkeling tours take visitors to some of the best spots around the island, including the Coral Garden and the Tiki Village.

Kayaking and paddleboarding are also popular ways to explore the lagoon. Many resorts and rental shops offer equipment, allowing visitors to paddle through the calm waters at their leisure. The clear waters provide excellent visibility, making it easy to spot marine life below. For a truly magical experience, consider a sunset paddle, where the sky transforms into a canvas of vibrant colors as the sun dips below the horizon.

Moorea's beaches are some of the most beautiful in French Polynesia. Temae Beach, located on the northeastern coast, is a favorite among locals and visitors alike. The long stretch of white sand and crystal-clear waters make it an ideal spot for swimming, sunbathing, and picnicking. Another popular beach is Ta'ahiamanu Beach, located near Opunohu Bay. This beach offers excellent snorkeling opportunities, with coral reefs just a short swim from the shore.

The island's rich cultural heritage is evident in its many marae (ancient Polynesian temples) and traditional villages. A visit to the Tiki Village Cultural Center provides a fascinating insight into Polynesian culture and history. The center offers demonstrations of traditional crafts, such as weaving and tattooing, as well as performances of Polynesian dance and music. The highlight of any visit is the evening show, which features fire dancing and a traditional feast known as a "tamaaraa."

Moorea's culinary scene is a delightful fusion of Polynesian, French, and international flavors. Fresh seafood is a staple, with dishes such as poisson cru (raw fish marinated in coconut milk and lime) and grilled mahi-mahi being popular choices. The island's many restaurants and food trucks, known as roulottes, offer a range of dining options to suit all tastes and budgets. For a special treat, consider dining at one of the island's gourmet restaurants, such as Le Mahogany or Moorea Beach Cafe, where you can enjoy exquisite cuisine in a stunning setting.

A visit to Moorea would not be complete without experiencing the island's vibrant marine life. Dolphin and whale watching tours are a highlight, offering the chance to see these magnificent creatures in their natural habitat. The waters around Moorea are home to a resident population of spinner dolphins, and humpback whales migrate to the area from July to November. These tours are led by knowledgeable guides who provide fascinating insights into the behavior and biology of these marine mammals.

For those seeking relaxation and rejuvenation, Moorea's spas offer a range of treatments inspired by Polynesian traditions. A massage using monoi oil, a fragrant blend of coconut oil and tiare flowers, is a soothing way to unwind. Many spas are located in stunning settings, such as overwater bungalows or beachfront pavilions, enhancing the sense of tranquility.

Shopping in Moorea provides the opportunity to purchase unique souvenirs and local crafts. The island's boutiques and markets offer a variety of items, from black pearls and handwoven hats to pareos (sarongs) and wood carvings. Black pearls, in particular, are a sought-after memento, with several reputable jewelers offering exquisite pieces.

Moorea's nightlife, while more subdued than some other destinations, offers a range of options for evening entertainment. Many resorts feature live music and traditional dance shows, providing a taste of Polynesian culture. For a more laid-back evening, enjoying a cocktail at a beachfront bar while watching the sunset is a perfect way to end the day.

The island's warm and welcoming people are an integral part of the Moorea experience. The genuine hospitality and friendliness of the locals create a sense of connection and make visitors feel at home. Engaging with the community, whether through a cultural tour or simply chatting with locals, enriches the travel experience and provides a deeper appreciation of the island's way of life.

Moorea, with its stunning natural beauty, luxurious accommodations, and rich cultural heritage, offers a magical escape that captivates the heart and soul. Whether you're exploring the vibrant marine life of the lagoon, savoring a gourmet meal under the stars, or simply relaxing on a pristine beach, the island provides a myriad of experiences that create lasting memories.

3.4 The Marquesas: Untamed Beauty

The Marquesas Islands, a remote archipelago in French Polynesia, are a world apart from the more frequented tourist destinations like Tahiti and Bora Bora. Known for their rugged landscapes, rich cultural heritage, and untamed beauty, the Marquesas offer an experience that is both raw and profoundly captivating.

The Marquesas are composed of twelve islands, six of which are inhabited. Each island has its own distinct character and charm, but they all share a common thread of dramatic landscapes and a deep connection to Polynesian culture. The islands are volcanic in origin, characterized by towering cliffs, lush valleys, and pristine beaches. The remoteness of the Marquesas has helped preserve their natural beauty and cultural traditions, making them a fascinating destination for those seeking an off-the-beaten-path adventure.

Nuku Hiva, the largest of the Marquesas Islands, serves as the administrative center and a gateway to the archipelago. The island's dramatic scenery includes towering cliffs, deep valleys, and cascading waterfalls. One of the most iconic landmarks is the Hakatea Bay, also known as Daniel's Bay, which is accessible by boat or a challenging hike. The bay is surrounded by steep cliffs and lush vegetation, creating a secluded paradise that feels worlds away from civilization. The hike to the Vaipo Waterfall, one of the tallest in French Polynesia, is a rewarding adventure that takes you through dense jungle and past ancient archaeological sites.

Exploring the island's interior reveals a wealth of cultural and historical treasures. The Taipivai Valley, made famous by Herman Melville's novel "Typee," is home to numerous archaeological sites, including ancient stone platforms (paepae), petroglyphs, and tiki statues. Guided tours provide valuable insights into the history and significance of these sites, offering a deeper understanding of the Marquesan way of life.

Hiva Oa, the second-largest island in the Marquesas, is renowned for its artistic heritage and as the final resting place of the French artist Paul Gauguin and Belgian singer Jacques Brel. The island's main village, Atuona, is home to the Paul Gauguin Cultural Center, which showcases the artist's life and works. Visitors can also pay their respects at the Calvary Cemetery, where both Gauguin and Brel are buried, their graves offering a poignant reminder of the island's allure to creative souls.

Hiva Oa is also rich in archaeological sites, with the Puamau Valley being a highlight. The valley is home to the largest tiki statues in French Polynesia, including the impressive Takaii, which stands over eight feet tall. These ancient stone figures, believed to represent deified ancestors, are a testament to the island's spiritual and cultural heritage. The nearby Lipona site features a collection of well-preserved tikis and stone platforms, providing a fascinating glimpse into the island's past.

Ua Pou, known for its distinctive basalt spires, is another must-visit island in the Marquesas. The island's dramatic peaks, including the iconic Poumaka and Poutetaunui, dominate the landscape and create a striking backdrop for exploration. The village of Hakahau, the island's main settlement, offers a warm welcome to visitors and serves as a base for exploring the island's natural and cultural attractions. The Hakahau Valley is home to several archaeological sites, including ancient petroglyphs and stone platforms, while the island's rugged terrain offers excellent hiking opportunities.

Ua Huka, one of the smaller islands in the Marquesas, is known for its wild horses and rich birdlife. The island's arid landscape contrasts with the lush greenery of its neighbors, creating a unique environment that is home to several endemic species. The village of Vaipaee is home to the Marquesan Museum, which houses an impressive collection of artifacts, including traditional tools, weapons, and carvings. The island's rugged coastline and secluded beaches offer opportunities for exploration and relaxation, while the interior is crisscrossed with hiking trails that lead to ancient archaeological sites.

Fatu Hiva, the southernmost island in the Marquesas, is often described as the most beautiful. The island's lush valleys, dramatic cliffs, and pristine beaches create a paradise for nature lovers. The village of Omoa is known for its traditional crafts, including tapa cloth and wood carvings, which make for unique souvenirs. The hike from Omoa to Hanavave, known as the "Bay of Virgins," is one of the most scenic in the Marquesas, offering breathtaking views of the island's rugged landscape and the azure waters of the Pacific.

Tahuata, the smallest inhabited island in the Marquesas, is known for its rich history and beautiful beaches. The island's main village, Vaitahu, was the site of the first European landing in the Marquesas, and its church, built by early missionaries, is a testament to this history. The island's white-sand beaches, such as Hana Moe Noa and Hapatoni, offer idyllic spots for swimming and relaxation, while the interior is home to several archaeological sites.

The Marquesas are not just about stunning landscapes and ancient history; they are also a place where traditional Polynesian culture thrives. The islands are known for their vibrant arts and crafts, including wood carving, tattooing, and weaving. Visitors have the opportunity to learn about these traditional practices and even participate in workshops led by local artisans. The Marquesan Festival, held every four years, is a celebration of the islands' cultural heritage, featuring traditional music, dance, and sports.

The cuisine of the Marquesas is a reflection of the islands' natural bounty and cultural influences. Fresh seafood, tropical fruits, and locally grown vegetables are staples, often prepared using traditional methods. A visit to a local market or a meal at a family-run restaurant offers a taste of authentic Marquesan flavors, from poisson cru (raw fish marinated in coconut milk and lime) to breadfruit and taro dishes.

Traveling to the Marquesas requires a sense of adventure and a willingness to embrace the islands' remote and rugged nature. The journey is part of the experience, whether arriving by plane or by sea. The islands' remoteness means that they are less developed than other parts of French Polynesia, but this only adds to their charm. Accommodations range from guesthouses and pensions to more luxurious options, all offering a warm welcome and a chance to immerse yourself in the local way of life.

The Marquesas Islands, with their untamed beauty and rich cultural heritage, offer a travel experience that is both unique and profoundly rewarding. From exploring ancient archaeological sites and hiking through lush valleys to experiencing traditional arts and savoring local cuisine, the Marquesas provide a journey into the heart of Polynesia that leaves a lasting impression.

3.5 The Tuamotus: Diver's Dream

The Tuamotu Archipelago, a vast chain of coral atolls stretching over the Pacific Ocean, is a diver's dream come true. With its crystal-clear waters, vibrant marine life, and stunning underwater landscapes, the Tuamotus offer an unparalleled diving experience.

The Tuamotus consist of 77 atolls, each with its own unique charm and underwater treasures. These atolls are characterized by their ring-shaped coral reefs encircling turquoise lagoons, creating a paradise for divers. The remoteness of the Tuamotus has helped preserve their pristine marine environments, making them a haven for a diverse array of marine species.

Rangiroa, the largest atoll in the Tuamotus and one of the largest in the world, is a premier diving destination. The atoll's lagoon is so vast that it could encompass the entire island of Tahiti. Rangiroa is renowned for its pass dives, where divers can experience the exhilarating rush of currents flowing through the narrow channels that connect the lagoon to the open ocean. The Tiputa Pass is particularly famous for its thrilling drift dives, where divers can encounter schools of sharks, manta rays, and dolphins. The Avatoru Pass, another popular dive site, offers the chance to see a variety of pelagic species, including barracudas and tuna.

The Blue Lagoon, located within Rangiroa's lagoon, is a must-visit for its stunning beauty and abundant marine life. The shallow, crystal-clear waters of the Blue Lagoon are perfect for snorkeling, allowing visitors to observe colorful coral gardens and a myriad of tropical fish. For those seeking a more immersive experience, diving in the Blue Lagoon offers the chance to see larger marine species, such as reef sharks and eagle rays.

Fakarava, another top diving destination in the Tuamotus, is a UNESCO Biosphere Reserve known for its exceptional biodiversity. The atoll's two main passes, Garuae and Tumakohua, are renowned for their rich marine life and spectacular coral formations. The Garuae Pass, the largest pass in French Polynesia, is famous for its "wall of sharks," where hundreds of grey reef sharks can be seen patrolling the currents. The Tumakohua Pass, also known as the South Pass, offers a more intimate diving experience, with vibrant coral gardens and a diverse array of marine species, including groupers, napoleon wrasses, and moray eels.

Fakarava's lagoon is also home to several unique dive sites, such as the "Shark Hole," where divers can observe a large congregation of nurse sharks resting on the sandy bottom. The "Coral City" dive site features an impressive array of coral formations, providing a stunning backdrop for encounters with reef fish, turtles, and rays. The atoll's pristine waters and abundant marine life make Fakarava a true paradise for divers.

Tikehau, often referred to as the "Pink Sand Island," is another gem in the Tuamotus. The atoll's lagoon is teeming with marine life, making it a popular destination for both diving and snorkeling. The Tuheiava Pass, the main pass in Tikehau, offers thrilling drift dives where divers can encounter schools of barracudas, eagle rays, and grey reef sharks. The atoll's coral gardens are home to a diverse array of tropical fish, including parrotfish, butterflyfish, and angelfish.

The "Manta Ray Cleaning Station" is a unique dive site in Tikehau, where divers can observe manta rays being cleaned by small wrasses and other cleaner fish. This fascinating behavior provides a rare opportunity to see these majestic creatures up close. The atoll's pink sand beaches, formed from crushed coral, add to the allure of Tikehau, making it a perfect destination for relaxation and underwater exploration.

Manihi, known for its black pearl farms, offers a unique diving experience that combines marine exploration with cultural immersion. The atoll's lagoon is dotted with pearl farms, where visitors can learn about the intricate process of cultivating black pearls. Diving in Manihi's lagoon offers the chance to see the pearl farms up close, as well as encounter a variety of marine species, including reef sharks, rays, and tropical fish. The atoll's coral reefs are home to vibrant coral gardens and an abundance of marine life, making it a rewarding destination for divers.

The Tuamotus are not just about diving; they also offer a range of other activities for visitors to enjoy. Snorkeling is a popular pastime, with the shallow lagoons providing the perfect environment for observing colorful coral gardens and tropical fish. Kayaking and paddleboarding are also great ways to explore the atolls' lagoons and coastline, offering a unique perspective on the stunning natural beauty of the Tuamotus.

For those interested in cultural experiences, the Tuamotus offer a glimpse into traditional Polynesian life. The atolls are home to small, close-knit communities that maintain a strong connection to their cultural heritage. Visitors can learn about traditional fishing techniques, sample local cuisine, and participate in cultural events and festivals. The warm hospitality of the Tuamotuans adds to the charm of these remote islands, making visitors feel welcome and at home.

Accommodations in the Tuamotus range from guesthouses and pensions to more luxurious options, all offering a chance to immerse yourself in the local way of life. Staying in a guesthouse or pension provides a more intimate and authentic experience, with the opportunity to interact with local families and learn about their customs and traditions. For those seeking more comfort, there are several resorts that offer a range of amenities and activities, including diving excursions, spa treatments, and gourmet dining.

Traveling to the Tuamotus requires a sense of adventure and a willingness to embrace the islands' remote and rugged nature. The journey is part of the experience, whether arriving by plane or by sea. The remoteness of the Tuamotus means that they are less developed than other parts of French Polynesia, but this only adds to their charm. The pristine natural beauty and rich marine life of the Tuamotus make them a truly unique and rewarding destination for divers and travelers alike.

The Tuamotu Archipelago, with its crystal-clear waters, vibrant marine life, and stunning underwater landscapes, offers a diving experience that is both exhilarating and profoundly rewarding. From the thrilling pass dives of Rangiroa and Fakarava to the serene coral gardens of Tikehau and Manihi, the Tuamotus provide a journey into the heart of the Pacific that leaves a lasting impression. Whether you are an experienced diver or a beginner, the Tuamotus offer an underwater paradise that is waiting to be explored.

3.6 The Australs and Gambier Archipelago: Hidden Gems

The Australs and Gambier Archipelago, often overshadowed by their more famous counterparts in French Polynesia, offer a treasure trove of hidden gems waiting to be discovered. These remote islands, with their unspoiled landscapes, rich cultural heritage, and unique biodiversity, provide an authentic and off-the-beaten-path experience for travelers seeking something truly special.

The Austral Islands, located to the south of Tahiti, consist of seven main islands: Rurutu, Tubuai, Rimatara, Raivavae, Rapa, and the uninhabited Maria and Marotiri. Each island boasts its own distinct charm and attractions, making the Australs a diverse and captivating destination.

Rurutu, known as the "Island of Whales," is famous for its annual humpback whale migration. From July to October, these majestic creatures can be seen in the waters surrounding the island, offering a unique opportunity for whale watching. The island's rugged coastline, with its dramatic cliffs and hidden caves, provides a stunning backdrop for this awe-inspiring spectacle. Rurutu's lush interior is dotted with ancient marae (sacred sites) and traditional villages, where visitors can learn about the island's rich cultural heritage and participate in local crafts such as weaving and tapa making.

Tubuai, the largest island in the Australs, is a haven for nature lovers and outdoor enthusiasts. The island's fertile valleys and rolling hills are perfect for hiking and exploring, with trails leading to panoramic viewpoints and hidden waterfalls. Tubuai's lagoon, with its crystal-clear waters and vibrant coral reefs, offers excellent snorkeling and diving opportunities. The island's rich history, including its role as a refuge for the mutineers of the HMS Bounty, adds an intriguing layer to its natural beauty.

Rimatara, the smallest inhabited island in the Australs, is a tranquil paradise known for its pristine beaches and traditional way of life. The island's isolation has helped preserve its unique flora and fauna, including the endangered Rimatara lorikeet, a brightly colored parrot found only on this island. Visitors to Rimatara can immerse themselves in the island's peaceful atmosphere, exploring its lush landscapes and interacting with the friendly local community.

Raivavae, often referred to as the "Bora Bora of the Australs," is renowned for its stunning lagoon and picturesque motus (islets). The island's turquoise waters and white sandy beaches rival those of its more famous counterpart, but with a fraction of the tourists. Raivavae's lagoon is perfect for swimming, snorkeling, and kayaking, while its interior offers hiking trails that lead to ancient archaeological sites and breathtaking viewpoints. The island's vibrant culture, with its traditional dances and crafts, adds to its allure.

Rapa, the southernmost island in the Australs, is a remote and rugged paradise that remains largely untouched by tourism. The island's dramatic landscapes, with their steep cliffs and verdant valleys, are perfect for adventurous travelers seeking solitude and natural beauty. Rapa's rich cultural heritage, including its unique dialect and traditional practices, provides a fascinating glimpse into the island's history and way of life. The island's isolation and limited infrastructure make it a challenging destination to reach, but those who make the journey are rewarded with an unforgettable experience.

The Gambier Archipelago, located to the southeast of Tahiti, consists of the main island of Mangareva and several smaller islands and atolls. The archipelago's remote location and pristine environment make it a hidden gem for travelers seeking an authentic and unspoiled destination.

Mangareva, the largest and most populous island in the Gambier Archipelago, is known for its rich history and stunning natural beauty. The island's lush landscapes, with their rolling hills and fertile valleys, are perfect for hiking and exploring. Mangareva's lagoon, with its crystal-clear waters and vibrant coral reefs, offers excellent snorkeling and diving opportunities. The island's rich cultural heritage, including its role as a center of Catholic missionary activity in the 19th century, adds an intriguing layer to its natural beauty. Visitors can explore the island's historic churches and convents, as well as its ancient marae and other archaeological sites.

The smaller islands and atolls of the Gambier Archipelago, such as Taravai, Akamaru, and Aukena, offer a more secluded and intimate experience. These islands are home to pristine beaches, vibrant coral reefs, and traditional villages, where visitors can immerse themselves in the local way of life. The archipelago's remote location and limited infrastructure make it a challenging destination to reach, but those who make the journey are rewarded with an unforgettable experience.

The Australs and Gambier Archipelago offer a range of activities for visitors to enjoy, from hiking and exploring to snorkeling and diving. The islands' unspoiled landscapes and rich cultural heritage provide a unique and authentic experience that is hard to find elsewhere. Whether you are seeking adventure, relaxation, or cultural immersion, the Australs and Gambier Archipelago have something to offer.

Accommodations in the Australs and Gambier Archipelago range from guesthouses and pensions to more luxurious options, all offering a chance to immerse yourself in the local way of life. Staying in a guesthouse or pension provides a more intimate and authentic experience, with the opportunity to interact with local families and learn about their customs and traditions. For those seeking more comfort, there are several resorts that offer a range of amenities and activities, including diving excursions, spa treatments, and gourmet dining.

Traveling to the Australs and Gambier Archipelago requires a sense of adventure and a willingness to embrace the islands' remote and rugged nature. The journey is part of the experience, whether arriving by plane or by sea. The remoteness of these islands means that they are less developed than other parts of French Polynesia, but this only adds to their charm. The pristine natural beauty and rich cultural heritage of the Australs and Gambier Archipelago make them a truly unique and rewarding destination for travelers seeking an authentic and off-the-beaten-path experience.

The Australs and Gambier Archipelago, with their unspoiled landscapes, rich cultural heritage, and unique biodiversity, offer a treasure trove of hidden gems waiting to be discovered. From the whale-watching opportunities of Rurutu to the stunning lagoon of Raivavae, the rugged beauty of Rapa, and the rich history of Mangareva, these remote islands provide an authentic and unforgettable experience for travelers seeking something truly special. Whether you are an adventurer, a nature lover, or a cultural enthusiast, the Australs and Gambier Archipelago have something to offer.

CHAPTER 4: CULTURAL EXPERIENCES

4.1 Traditional Polynesian Festivals

Polynesian festivals are a vibrant tapestry of music, dance, and tradition, offering a window into the soul of French Polynesia. These celebrations, deeply rooted in the islands' history and culture, provide an immersive experience for travelers eager to connect with the local way of life. From the grand Heiva i Tahiti to the intimate village gatherings, each festival is a unique expression of Polynesian identity and community spirit.

Heiva i Tahiti, the most famous and grandiose of all Polynesian festivals, takes place annually in July. This month-long celebration in Papeete, the capital of Tahiti, is a spectacular showcase of traditional dance, music, and sports. The origins of Heiva date back to ancient times when Polynesians would gather to honor their gods and celebrate significant events. Today, it remains a powerful expression of cultural pride and resilience.

The heart of Heiva i Tahiti lies in its dance competitions, where groups from different islands perform intricate routines that tell stories of love, war, and nature. These performances, known as 'ori Tahiti, are a mesmerizing blend of rhythmic drumming, graceful movements, and elaborate costumes adorned with feathers, shells, and tapa cloth. The dancers' synchronized steps and expressive gestures convey a deep connection to their heritage, captivating audiences with their passion and skill.

Music is another integral part of Heiva i Tahiti, with traditional instruments such as the pahu (drum), vivo (nose flute), and ukulele providing the soundtrack to the festivities. The songs, often sung in the Tahitian language, recount legends and historical events, preserving the oral traditions of the islands. The music's infectious rhythms and melodies invite everyone to join in the celebration, creating a sense of unity and joy.

In addition to dance and music, Heiva i Tahiti features a variety of traditional sports and games that showcase the physical prowess and competitive spirit of the Polynesian people. Events such as stone lifting, coconut tree climbing, and outrigger canoe races draw enthusiastic crowds, cheering on the athletes as they demonstrate their strength and agility. These competitions, rooted in ancient practices, highlight the importance of physical fitness and endurance in Polynesian culture.

While Heiva i Tahiti is the most well-known festival, numerous other celebrations take place throughout French Polynesia, each offering a unique glimpse into the islands' diverse cultural landscape. The Marquesas Islands, for example, host the biennial Matavaa festival, a gathering of artists, musicians, and dancers from across the archipelago. This event, held in December, celebrates the rich artistic heritage of the Marquesas, with performances and exhibitions that showcase the islands' distinctive tattooing, carving, and weaving traditions.

The Tuamotu Archipelago, known for its stunning atolls and lagoons, also has its own unique festivals. The Hawaiki Nui Va'a, an annual outrigger canoe race held in November, is one of the most prestigious events in the region. Teams from around the world compete in this grueling three-day race, paddling across the open ocean between the islands of Huahine, Raiatea, Taha'a, and Bora Bora. The race not only tests the participants' endurance and skill but also honors the ancient Polynesian tradition of voyaging and navigation.

In the Austral Islands, the Taputapuatea festival on the island of Raivavae is a celebration of the region's spiritual heritage. Held in October, this event brings together communities from across the Australs to honor their ancestors and the sacred marae (temples) that dot the landscape. The festival includes traditional ceremonies, dance performances, and storytelling sessions that highlight the deep spiritual connection between the people and their land.

The Gambier Islands, with their remote location and rich history, offer a more intimate festival experience. The Mangareva Pearl Festival, held in August, celebrates the islands' renowned black pearl industry. Visitors can tour pearl farms, learn about the cultivation process, and purchase exquisite jewelry crafted from these lustrous gems. The festival also features cultural performances, traditional food, and craft demonstrations, providing a well-rounded introduction to the unique heritage of the Gambier Islands.

Participating in these festivals offers travelers a deeper understanding of Polynesian culture and a chance to connect with the local community. To make the most of these experiences, it's essential to approach them with respect and an open mind. Learning a few basic phrases in the local language, dressing modestly, and observing local customs can go a long way in showing appreciation for the culture and fostering positive interactions.

Travelers should also be mindful of the environmental impact of their visit. Many of the islands in French Polynesia are fragile ecosystems, and it's crucial to minimize waste, conserve resources, and support sustainable tourism practices. By doing so, visitors can help preserve the natural beauty and cultural heritage of these islands for future generations.

In addition to the major festivals, smaller village celebrations and family gatherings offer a more intimate glimpse into Polynesian life. These events, often centered around important milestones such as weddings, births, and religious ceremonies, provide an opportunity to experience the warmth and hospitality of the local community. Visitors who are fortunate enough to be invited to such gatherings should consider it a privilege and honor, as these occasions are deeply personal and significant.

Traditional Polynesian festivals are a vibrant and essential part of the cultural fabric of French Polynesia. From the grand spectacle of Heiva i Tahiti to the intimate village celebrations, these events offer a unique and immersive experience for travelers seeking to connect with the local way of life. By participating in these festivals with respect and an open mind, visitors can gain a deeper appreciation for the rich heritage and enduring spirit of the Polynesian people.

4.2 Local Music and Dance

The rhythmic pulse of drums, the melodic strumming of ukuleles, and the graceful sway of dancers' hips—these are the sights and sounds that define the cultural heartbeat of Tahiti and French Polynesia. Music and dance are not mere forms of entertainment here; they are integral to the islands' identity, a living testament to their rich history and vibrant traditions. For travelers, immersing in these local art forms offers a profound connection to the spirit of the islands.

Traditional Polynesian music is a captivating blend of vocal harmonies and instrumental rhythms. The pahu, a large wooden drum, serves as the backbone of many musical compositions. Its deep, resonant beats set the tempo for dances and ceremonies, creating an atmosphere that is both powerful and mesmerizing. Accompanying the pahu is the to'ere, a slit drum made from hollowed-out tree trunks. The to'ere produces sharp, staccato sounds that add complexity and texture to the music.

The ukulele, though often associated with Hawaiian music, is also a staple in Polynesian musical traditions. This small, four-stringed instrument produces a bright, cheerful sound that complements the deeper tones of the drums. Ukulele players often strum intricate patterns, creating a lively and engaging musical backdrop for both casual gatherings and formal performances.

Vocal music in Polynesia is equally enchanting. Traditional songs, known as himene, are often performed in groups, with singers harmonizing in rich, layered arrangements. These songs can be celebratory, spiritual, or even humorous, reflecting the diverse experiences and emotions of the Polynesian people. The lyrics, usually in the Tahitian language, tell stories of love, nature, and ancestral legends, preserving the oral history of the islands.

Dance, or 'ori Tahiti, is perhaps the most visually striking aspect of Polynesian culture. This traditional dance form is characterized by fluid, expressive movements that convey a wide range of emotions and narratives. Female dancers, adorned in colorful pareos and elaborate headdresses, perform graceful hip movements and hand gestures that mimic the natural world. Male dancers, on the other hand, showcase powerful, energetic motions that demonstrate strength and agility.

One of the most iconic dances is the otea, a fast-paced performance that features synchronized movements and intricate choreography. The otea is often accompanied by live drumming, with the dancers' movements perfectly timed to the rhythmic beats. This dance is typically performed at festivals, ceremonies, and other special occasions, captivating audiences with its intensity and precision.

Another popular dance is the aparima, a slower, more lyrical performance that focuses on storytelling through hand gestures. The name "aparima" translates to "kiss of the hands," highlighting the importance of the dancers' expressive movements. In an aparima, dancers use their hands to depict scenes from daily life, such as fishing, weaving, or planting. This dance is often accompanied by melodic ukulele music and soft drumming, creating a serene and evocative atmosphere.

For travelers seeking to experience Polynesian music and dance firsthand, there are numerous opportunities to do so. Many hotels and resorts offer cultural shows that feature traditional performances, providing a convenient and accessible way to enjoy these art forms. These shows often include a variety of dances and musical numbers, giving visitors a well-rounded introduction to Polynesian culture.

However, for a more authentic and immersive experience, travelers should consider attending local festivals and community events. These gatherings offer a chance to see traditional performances in their natural context, surrounded by the warmth and hospitality of the local community. Events such as Heiva i Tahiti, the Marquesas Arts Festival, and the Hawaiki Nui Va'a canoe race often feature live music and dance, showcasing the talents of local artists and performers.

Participating in a dance workshop or music class is another excellent way to connect with Polynesian culture. Many local organizations and cultural centers offer lessons in 'ori Tahiti, ukulele playing, and drumming, allowing visitors to learn from skilled practitioners. These classes provide a hands-on experience, giving travelers a deeper appreciation for the skill and dedication required to master these art forms.

When attending performances or participating in workshops, it's important to approach these experiences with respect and an open mind. Understanding the cultural significance of the music and dance can enhance the experience, allowing travelers to fully appreciate the artistry and tradition behind each performance. Learning a few basic phrases in Tahitian, dressing appropriately, and observing local customs can also help foster positive interactions and show appreciation for the culture.

Beyond the traditional, contemporary Polynesian music and dance are also thriving, blending ancient influences with modern styles. Local musicians and dancers are experimenting with genres such as reggae, hip-hop, and electronic music, creating innovative and exciting new sounds. These contemporary expressions of Polynesian culture can be experienced at local bars, clubs, and music festivals, offering a fresh perspective on the islands' artistic landscape.

Exploring the local music and dance scene in Tahiti and French Polynesia is a journey into the heart of the islands' cultural heritage. From the powerful beats of the pahu drum to the graceful movements of 'ori Tahiti dancers, these art forms offer a window into the soul of Polynesia. By engaging with these traditions, travelers can forge a deeper connection to the islands and their people, creating lasting memories and a greater understanding of this unique and vibrant culture.

4.3 Art and Handicrafts

The vibrant colors of Tahitian pareos, the intricate patterns of Marquesan tattoos, and the delicate craftsmanship of pearl jewelry—these are just a few examples of the rich artistic traditions that thrive in Tahiti and French Polynesia. Art and handicrafts in this region are not merely decorative; they are deeply rooted in the islands' history, culture, and daily life. For travelers, exploring these artistic expressions offers a unique window into the soul of Polynesia.

One of the most iconic forms of Polynesian art is the tattoo, or tatau. This ancient practice dates back thousands of years and holds significant cultural and spiritual meaning. Tattoos were traditionally used to signify social status, achievements, and rites of passage. Each design is unique, often incorporating symbols and motifs that tell a personal story. The process of getting a tattoo is a sacred ritual, performed by skilled artists using traditional tools made from bone or shell. Today, many visitors choose to get a Polynesian tattoo as a meaningful souvenir, a permanent reminder of their connection to the islands.

Another quintessential Polynesian art form is the creation of pareos, or sarongs. These versatile garments are made from lightweight fabric, often adorned with vibrant, hand-painted designs. Pareos can be worn in numerous ways, serving as skirts, dresses, shawls, or even beach towels. The designs typically feature bold, tropical motifs such as hibiscus flowers, palm leaves, and marine life. Local artisans use a variety of techniques to create these patterns, including block printing, tie-dye, and batik. Purchasing a pareo directly from an artisan not only supports the local economy but also provides a unique and functional piece of wearable art.

Wood carving is another prominent craft in Polynesia, with each island group having its own distinct style. In the Marquesas Islands, for example, artisans are renowned for their intricate carvings of tiki figures. These statues, often made from wood or stone, represent deified ancestors and are believed to offer protection and guidance. The tiki figures are characterized by their bold, geometric patterns and expressive features. In contrast, the wood carvings of the Austral Islands often depict marine life and natural elements, reflecting the islanders' deep connection to the sea.

Basket weaving is a traditional craft that has been passed down through generations. Using natural materials such as pandanus leaves, coconut fibers, and bamboo, artisans create a variety of functional and decorative items. These include baskets, mats, hats, and fans, each meticulously woven by hand. The weaving techniques and patterns vary from island to island, with some regions known for their particularly fine and intricate work. Visitors can often watch artisans at work in local markets or cultural centers, gaining insight into the skill and patience required to produce these beautiful items.

Pearl jewelry is perhaps one of the most sought-after handicrafts in French Polynesia. The islands are famous for their black pearls, which are cultivated in the pristine lagoons of the Tuamotu and Gambier archipelagos. These pearls are prized for their unique colors, which can range from deep black to shades of green, blue, and even pink. Local jewelers create stunning pieces that showcase the natural beauty of these pearls, often incorporating them into necklaces, earrings, and bracelets. Visiting a pearl farm offers a fascinating glimpse into the cultivation process, from the seeding of the oysters to the harvesting and grading of the pearls.

For those interested in contemporary art, Tahiti and French Polynesia boast a thriving artistic community. Local galleries and studios showcase the work of modern Polynesian artists, who draw inspiration from their cultural heritage while experimenting with new styles and mediums. Paintings, sculptures, and mixed-media pieces often explore themes of identity, tradition, and the natural environment. Attending an art exhibition or visiting an artist's studio provides an opportunity to engage with the creative minds shaping the islands' artistic landscape.

Exploring local markets is one of the best ways to discover the diverse range of Polynesian art and handicrafts. The Papeete Market in Tahiti, for example, is a bustling hub where artisans from across the islands come to sell their wares. Here, visitors can find everything from hand-carved wooden bowls and shell jewelry to woven hats and colorful pareos. The market is also a great place to sample local delicacies and experience the lively atmosphere of Polynesian commerce.

When purchasing art and handicrafts, it's important to consider the authenticity and origin of the items. Supporting local artisans not only ensures that you are getting a genuine piece of Polynesian culture but also helps to sustain traditional crafts and provide income for the community. Look for items that are handmade using local materials and techniques, and don't be afraid to ask the artisans about their work. Many are happy to share the stories and meanings behind their creations, adding an extra layer of significance to your purchase.

For a deeper understanding of Polynesian art, visiting museums and cultural centers can be incredibly enriching. The Museum of Tahiti and Her Islands, located in Punaauia, offers a comprehensive overview of the region's history and culture, with extensive collections of traditional artifacts, including tools, clothing, and ceremonial objects. The Gauguin Museum, also in Tahiti, celebrates the life and work of the famous French painter who was inspired by the islands' beauty and culture. These institutions provide valuable context and insight into the artistic traditions of Polynesia.

Engaging with the art and handicrafts of Tahiti and French Polynesia is a journey into the heart of the islands' cultural heritage. Each piece, whether it's a tattoo, a pareo, or a carved tiki, tells a story of the land and its people. By appreciating and supporting these artistic expressions, travelers can forge a deeper connection to the islands and take home a piece of Polynesian soul.

4.4 Polynesian Cuisine

The culinary landscape of Tahiti and French Polynesia is a vibrant tapestry woven from the islands' rich natural resources, cultural influences, and traditional practices. Polynesian cuisine is a feast for the senses, offering a delightful blend of flavors, textures, and aromas that reflect the region's unique heritage. For travelers, exploring the local food scene is an essential part of experiencing the islands' culture.

One of the most iconic dishes in Polynesian cuisine is poisson cru, also known as ia ota. This dish is a Polynesian take on ceviche, featuring raw fish marinated in a mixture of lime juice and coconut milk. The fish, typically tuna, is cut into bite-sized pieces and combined with diced vegetables such as tomatoes, cucumbers, and onions. The lime juice "cooks" the fish, giving it a tender texture, while the coconut milk adds a creamy richness. Poisson cru is often served as an appetizer or a light main course, and its refreshing flavors make it a perfect dish for the tropical climate.

Another staple of Polynesian cuisine is the use of taro, a starchy root vegetable that has been cultivated in the region for centuries. Taro is incredibly versatile and can be prepared in various ways, including boiling, baking, and frying. One popular dish is po'e, a traditional dessert made from taro, coconut milk, and fruit such as bananas or papayas. The ingredients are mashed together and baked until they form a pudding-like consistency. Po'e is often served with a drizzle of coconut cream, adding a touch of sweetness and richness.

Breadfruit, known locally as uru, is another important ingredient in Polynesian cooking. This large, green fruit has a texture similar to potatoes and can be used in both savory and sweet dishes. One traditional preparation is to roast the breadfruit over an open fire until the skin is charred and the flesh is soft. The roasted breadfruit is then peeled and mashed, often served with coconut milk or used as a base for other dishes. Breadfruit can also be sliced and fried to make chips, providing a crunchy snack that pairs well with various dips and sauces.

The abundance of fresh seafood in French Polynesia is a testament to the islands' close relationship with the ocean. Fish, shellfish, and crustaceans are central to the local diet, and there are countless ways to prepare and enjoy them. Grilled fish, often marinated in a mixture of lime juice, garlic, and herbs, is a popular choice. Another traditional dish is mahi mahi, a type of fish that is often baked or grilled and served with a sauce made from coconut milk, lime juice, and spices. For a truly unique experience, travelers can try fafa, a dish made from chicken or pork cooked with taro leaves and coconut milk, resulting in a rich and flavorful stew.

Polynesian cuisine also features a variety of tropical fruits that thrive in the islands' fertile soil. Pineapples, mangoes, papayas, and bananas are just a few examples of the fruits that are enjoyed fresh or used in various dishes. One popular dessert is poe, a sweet pudding made from mashed fruit, coconut milk, and starch, often served with a drizzle of caramel sauce. Another favorite is the coconut bread, a sweet and dense bread made with grated coconut and coconut milk, often enjoyed as a snack or breakfast item.

The influence of French cuisine is also evident in the culinary traditions of Tahiti and French Polynesia. The islands' colonial history has left a lasting impact on the local food scene, resulting in a unique fusion of Polynesian and French flavors. Baguettes, croissants, and pastries are commonly found in local bakeries, and many restaurants offer dishes that blend French techniques with Polynesian ingredients. For example, poisson cru may be served with a side of French bread, or a traditional French dish like coq au vin might be prepared with local spices and flavors.

Street food is an integral part of the culinary experience in French Polynesia, offering a convenient and affordable way to sample a variety of local dishes. Food trucks, known as roulottes, are a common sight in towns and cities, particularly in Papeete, the capital of Tahiti. These mobile eateries serve a range of dishes, from grilled meats and seafood to crepes and sandwiches. One popular street food item is the casse-croûte, a sandwich made with a baguette and filled with ingredients such as ham, cheese, and vegetables. Another favorite is the chao men, a Polynesian take on Chinese chow mein, featuring stir-fried noodles with vegetables and meat or seafood.

For those looking to immerse themselves in the local food culture, visiting a traditional Polynesian feast, or tama'ara'a, is a must. These communal meals are often held to celebrate special occasions and feature a lavish spread of dishes prepared using traditional methods. One highlight of a tama'ara'a is the ahima'a, an underground oven used to cook a variety of foods. The oven is made by digging a pit in the ground and lining it with hot stones. Meat, fish, and vegetables are wrapped in banana leaves and placed in the pit, which is then covered with more leaves and earth. The food is left to cook slowly for several hours, resulting in tender, flavorful dishes infused with a smoky aroma.

Cooking classes offer another way for travelers to engage with Polynesian cuisine. Many local chefs and culinary schools offer classes that teach participants how to prepare traditional dishes using fresh, local ingredients. These hands-on experiences provide valuable insights into the techniques and flavors that define Polynesian cooking, allowing travelers to take a piece of the islands' culinary heritage home with them.

Exploring the markets is an essential part of experiencing Polynesian cuisine. The Papeete Market, also known as Le Marché, is a bustling hub where vendors sell a wide array of fresh produce, seafood, and prepared foods. Visitors can sample local delicacies such as poisson cru, grilled fish, and tropical fruits, while also picking up ingredients to try their hand at cooking Polynesian dishes. The market is also a great place to find handmade crafts and souvenirs, making it a one-stop destination for both food and culture.

Polynesian cuisine is a reflection of the islands' rich cultural heritage and natural abundance. Each dish tells a story of the land and its people, offering a taste of the traditions and flavors that have been passed down through generations. By exploring the local food scene, travelers can gain a deeper appreciation for the islands' unique culinary identity and create lasting memories of their time in Tahiti and French Polynesia.

4.5 Engaging with Local Communities

Engaging with local communities in Tahiti and French Polynesia offers travelers a unique opportunity to immerse themselves in the rich cultural tapestry of the islands. The warmth and hospitality of the Polynesian people, combined with their deep-rooted traditions and customs, create an enriching experience that goes beyond the typical tourist attractions. By connecting with the locals, visitors can gain a deeper understanding of the islands' way of life, history, and values.

One of the most authentic ways to engage with local communities is by participating in traditional ceremonies and festivals. These events are often vibrant and colorful, showcasing the islands' cultural heritage through music, dance, and rituals. The Heiva i Tahiti, held annually in July, is one of the most significant cultural festivals in French Polynesia. This month-long celebration features traditional dance competitions, music performances, and sporting events, providing a window into the islands' rich cultural traditions. Visitors are welcome to join in the festivities, whether by watching the performances, participating in workshops, or simply mingling with the locals.

Another meaningful way to connect with the local community is by visiting small villages and spending time with the residents. Many villages in French Polynesia have preserved their traditional way of life, offering a glimpse into the daily routines and customs of the Polynesian people. In these villages, visitors can observe traditional crafts such as weaving, carving, and tattooing. Engaging with artisans and learning about their techniques and the cultural significance of their work can be a deeply rewarding experience. Some villages also offer homestay programs, allowing travelers to live with a local family and experience their way of life firsthand.

Language plays a crucial role in connecting with local communities. While French is the official language of French Polynesia, many residents also speak Tahitian and other Polynesian languages. Learning a few basic phrases in Tahitian can go a long way in building rapport with the locals. Simple greetings, expressions of gratitude, and polite inquiries can help break the ice and show respect for the local culture. Many locals appreciate the effort and are more likely to engage in meaningful conversations when visitors make an attempt to speak their language.

Participating in community-based tourism initiatives is another excellent way to engage with local communities. These initiatives are designed to benefit the local population by promoting sustainable tourism practices and preserving cultural heritage. One such initiative is the Tetiaroa Society, which offers eco-tours and educational programs on the atoll of Tetiaroa. Visitors can learn about the island's unique ecosystem, conservation efforts, and the cultural history of the area. By supporting community-based tourism, travelers can contribute to the well-being of the local population while gaining a deeper appreciation for the islands' natural and cultural heritage.

Volunteering is another impactful way to connect with local communities. Various organizations in French Polynesia offer volunteer programs that focus on environmental conservation, education, and community development. For example, visitors can participate in beach cleanups, coral reef restoration projects, or educational programs for local children. Volunteering not only provides an opportunity to give back to the community but also fosters meaningful connections with the locals and a deeper understanding of the challenges they face.

Exploring local markets is a fantastic way to engage with the community and experience the vibrant culture of French Polynesia. Markets such as the Papeete Market, also known as Le Marché, are bustling hubs where locals gather to sell and buy fresh produce, handmade crafts, and traditional foods. Visitors can interact with vendors, sample local delicacies, and purchase unique souvenirs. The lively atmosphere of the markets offers a glimpse into the daily life of the Polynesian people and provides an opportunity to support local artisans and farmers.

Attending cultural workshops and classes is another way to engage with the local community and learn about Polynesian traditions. Many cultural centers and organizations offer workshops on traditional dance, music, cooking, and crafts. For example, visitors can take a dance class to learn the graceful movements of the Tahitian dance, or 'Ori Tahiti, which is an integral part of Polynesian culture. Cooking classes offer a hands-on experience in preparing traditional dishes such as poisson cru and coconut bread. These workshops provide valuable insights into the cultural practices of the islands and allow travelers to take a piece of Polynesian heritage home with them.

Respecting local customs and traditions is essential when engaging with local communities. Polynesian culture places a strong emphasis on respect, hospitality, and community. Visitors should be mindful of local etiquette, such as removing shoes before entering a home, dressing modestly, and asking for permission before taking photographs of people or sacred sites. Demonstrating respect for local customs fosters positive interactions and helps build trust and mutual understanding between visitors and the local community.

Storytelling is a cherished tradition in Polynesian culture, and listening to the stories of the locals can be a powerful way to connect with the community. Elders and cultural practitioners often share tales of the islands' history, mythology, and ancestral heritage. These stories provide valuable insights into the values, beliefs, and experiences of the Polynesian people. Engaging in conversations with storytellers and cultural practitioners can deepen one's appreciation for the rich oral traditions of the islands.

Supporting local businesses and artisans is another way to engage with the community and contribute to the local economy. Purchasing handmade crafts, locally produced foods, and other products directly from artisans and small businesses helps sustain traditional practices and supports the livelihoods of local families. Visitors can find unique items such as woven baskets, tapa cloth, and black pearl jewelry, each with its own cultural significance and story.

Engaging with local communities in Tahiti and French Polynesia offers a wealth of opportunities to experience the islands' culture in a meaningful and authentic way. By participating in traditional ceremonies, visiting villages, learning the language, supporting community-based tourism, volunteering, exploring markets, attending workshops, respecting customs, listening to stories, and supporting local businesses, travelers can forge lasting connections with the Polynesian people. These interactions enrich the travel experience and create lasting memories, fostering a deeper understanding and appreciation of the islands' unique cultural heritage.

CHAPTER 5: OUTDOOR ADVENTURES

5.1 Hiking and Trekking Trails

Tahiti and French Polynesia offer a paradise for outdoor enthusiasts, with a diverse range of hiking and trekking trails that showcase the islands' stunning landscapes and natural beauty. From lush rainforests and cascading waterfalls to volcanic peaks and coastal vistas, the trails provide an immersive experience for those seeking adventure and a deeper connection with nature.

One of the most iconic hiking destinations in Tahiti is Mount Aorai, the third-highest peak on the island. The trail to the summit of Mount Aorai is challenging but rewarding, offering breathtaking panoramic views of the island and the surrounding ocean. The hike begins at the Belvedere lookout, located at an elevation of 600 meters, and ascends through dense forest and rugged terrain. Along the way, hikers will encounter a variety of flora and fauna, including endemic species unique to Tahiti. The trail is well-marked, with several rest stops and shelters where hikers can take a break and enjoy the scenery. Reaching the summit, at an elevation of 2,066 meters, provides a sense of accomplishment and a stunning vantage point to admire the island's natural beauty.

For those seeking a less strenuous hike, the Fautaua Valley offers a picturesque and accessible option. The trail leads to the Fautaua Waterfall, one of the tallest waterfalls in Tahiti, with a drop of over 300 meters. The hike begins near the town of Papeete and follows a well-maintained path through lush vegetation and along the Fautaua River. The sound of rushing water and the sight of vibrant tropical plants create a serene and enchanting atmosphere. The trail culminates at the base of the waterfall, where hikers can take a refreshing dip in the natural pool and marvel at the sheer power and beauty of the cascading water.

On the island of Moorea, the Three Coconuts Pass is a popular hiking trail that offers stunning views of the island's dramatic landscape. The trail begins at the Belvedere lookout, which provides a panoramic view of Cook's Bay and Opunohu Bay. From there, the path winds through dense forest and up to the pass, where hikers are rewarded with sweeping vistas of the island's volcanic peaks and lush valleys. The hike is moderately challenging, with some steep sections, but the well-marked trail and the breathtaking scenery make it a worthwhile adventure.

For a unique hiking experience, the island of Huahine offers the Maeva Archaeological Site trail. This trail combines natural beauty with cultural and historical significance, as it leads hikers through ancient Polynesian ruins and sacred sites. The trail begins near the village of Maeva and follows a path along the shore of Lake Fauna Nui. Along the way, hikers will encounter stone marae (temples), ancient fish traps, and other archaeological remnants that provide a glimpse into the island's rich history and cultural heritage. The trail is relatively easy, making it suitable for hikers of all skill levels, and the combination of natural and cultural attractions makes it a fascinating and enriching experience.

On the island of Bora Bora, the Mount Pahia trail offers a challenging and exhilarating hike to one of the island's highest peaks. The trail begins near the village of Vaitape and ascends steeply through dense jungle and rocky terrain. The hike is strenuous, with some sections requiring scrambling and the use of ropes, but the effort is rewarded with spectacular views of Bora Bora's iconic lagoon and the surrounding islands. The summit of Mount Pahia, at an elevation of 661 meters, provides a breathtaking vantage point to admire the island's stunning beauty and the vibrant colors of the lagoon.

For those looking to explore the remote and pristine landscapes of the Marquesas Islands, the hike to the Vaipo Waterfall on the island of Nuku Hiva is a must. The trail begins in the village of Hakaui and follows a path through lush valleys and along the Hakaui River. The hike is moderately challenging, with some river crossings and steep sections, but the reward is the sight of the Vaipo Waterfall, one of the tallest waterfalls in French Polynesia, with a drop of over 350 meters. The remote and untouched beauty of the Marquesas Islands, combined with the dramatic scenery of the waterfall, makes this hike a truly unforgettable experience.

On the island of Raiatea, the hike to the summit of Mount Temehani offers a unique opportunity to explore the island's diverse ecosystems and endemic species. The trail begins near the village of Uturoa and ascends through a variety of landscapes, including dense forest, open meadows, and rocky ridges. Along the way, hikers will encounter a variety of plant and animal species, including the rare Tiare Apetahi, a flower that is found only on Mount Temehani. The summit, at an elevation of 772 meters, provides panoramic views of Raiatea and the surrounding islands, as well as a sense of connection to the island's natural heritage.

For a coastal hiking experience, the island of Tahaa offers the Tiva Coastal Trail, which follows a path along the island's rugged coastline. The trail begins near the village of Tiva and follows a path through coconut groves, along sandy beaches, and past rocky cliffs. The hike is relatively easy, with gentle terrain and well-marked paths, making it suitable for hikers of all skill levels. The coastal scenery, with its turquoise waters, white sandy beaches, and swaying palm trees, creates a picturesque and tranquil atmosphere.

Engaging in hiking and trekking in Tahiti and French Polynesia provides an opportunity to connect with the islands' natural beauty and diverse landscapes. Whether exploring volcanic peaks, lush valleys, ancient ruins, or pristine coastlines, the trails offer a sense of adventure and discovery. Each hike presents its own unique challenges and rewards, from the breathtaking views at the summit of Mount Aorai to the serene beauty of the Fautaua Waterfall. By immersing oneself in the natural environment and embracing the spirit of exploration, travelers can create lasting memories and a deeper appreciation for the islands' extraordinary landscapes.

5.2 Snorkeling and Diving Spots

The underwater world of Tahiti and French Polynesia is a mesmerizing realm teeming with vibrant marine life, colorful coral reefs, and crystal-clear waters. Snorkeling and diving in these islands offer unparalleled opportunities to explore this aquatic paradise, making it a must-do activity for any visitor. Whether you're a seasoned diver or a beginner, the diverse range of snorkeling and diving spots ensures that there's something for everyone.

One of the most renowned diving destinations in French Polynesia is the island of Rangiroa, part of the Tuamotu Archipelago. Known for its immense lagoon, Rangiroa is home to the famous Tiputa Pass, a natural channel that connects the lagoon to the open ocean. Diving in Tiputa Pass is an exhilarating experience, as the strong currents attract a plethora of marine life, including sharks, dolphins, manta rays, and schools of colorful fish. The drift dive through the pass allows divers to glide effortlessly with the current, providing a thrilling and unforgettable underwater adventure. For those who prefer snorkeling, the shallow areas of the lagoon offer a chance to observe vibrant coral gardens and a variety of tropical fish.

On the island of Bora Bora, the lagoon is a haven for snorkelers and divers alike. The Coral Gardens, located near the island's eastern coast, is a popular snorkeling spot known for its stunning coral formations and abundant marine life. The shallow waters make it an ideal location for beginners, while the diverse array of fish, including parrotfish, butterflyfish, and clownfish, ensures a captivating experience for all. For divers, the Anau dive site offers the opportunity to encounter majestic manta rays. These gentle giants are often seen gliding gracefully through the water, providing a breathtaking sight for those lucky enough to witness them.

The island of Moorea, with its dramatic landscapes and crystal-clear waters, is another top destination for snorkeling and diving. The Lagoonarium, a natural aquarium located on a small motu (islet) off the coast of Moorea, offers a unique snorkeling experience. Visitors can swim with a variety of marine life, including rays, sharks, and colorful fish, in a safe and controlled environment. For divers, the Tiki Point dive site is a must-visit. Known for its impressive coral formations and diverse marine life, Tiki Point offers the chance to see reef sharks, turtles, and a myriad of tropical fish. The clear visibility and calm waters make it an ideal spot for both novice and experienced divers.

On the island of Tahiti, the waters surrounding the island offer a range of snorkeling and diving opportunities. The Aquarium, located near the town of Punaauia, is a popular snorkeling spot known for its clear waters and abundant marine life. The shallow reef is home to a variety of fish, including angelfish, triggerfish, and surgeonfish, making it a great location for families and beginners. For divers, the wreck of the cargo ship "Nordby" offers a fascinating underwater exploration. The ship, which sank in 1900, lies at a depth of 30 meters and is now covered in coral and inhabited by a variety of marine life. Exploring the wreck provides a unique glimpse into the island's maritime history and the underwater world.

The island of Fakarava, another gem in the Tuamotu Archipelago, is a UNESCO Biosphere Reserve known for its pristine coral reefs and rich marine biodiversity. The Garuae Pass, the largest pass in French Polynesia, is a renowned diving spot that attracts divers from around the world. The strong currents in the pass create a dynamic underwater environment, teeming with sharks, rays, and schools of fish. The drift dive through Garuae Pass is an exhilarating experience, offering the chance to see a variety of marine life up close. For snorkelers, the shallow areas of the lagoon provide a tranquil and picturesque setting to observe coral gardens and tropical fish.

On the island of Huahine, the Avea Bay offers a serene and beautiful snorkeling experience. The calm and clear waters of the bay are home to a variety of marine life, including rays, turtles, and colorful fish. The shallow reef is easily accessible from the shore, making it an ideal spot for beginners and families. For divers, the Fitii Canyon dive site offers the chance to explore underwater canyons and coral formations. The diverse marine life, including reef sharks, barracudas, and moray eels, ensures an exciting and memorable dive.

The island of Tikehau, with its pink sand beaches and turquoise waters, is another top destination for snorkeling and diving. The Tuheiava Pass, the main pass into the lagoon, is a renowned diving spot known for its rich marine biodiversity. The pass is home to a variety of marine life, including sharks, rays, and schools of fish, making it a thrilling dive for experienced divers. For snorkelers, the shallow areas of the lagoon offer a chance to observe vibrant coral gardens and a variety of tropical fish in a tranquil and picturesque setting.

Engaging in snorkeling and diving in Tahiti and French Polynesia provides an opportunity to connect with the islands' underwater beauty and diverse marine life. Whether exploring the vibrant coral gardens of Bora Bora, drifting through the exhilarating passes of Rangiroa and Fakarava, or observing the gentle manta rays of Moorea, the underwater adventures in these islands are truly unparalleled. Each snorkeling and diving spot offers its own unique challenges and rewards, from the breathtaking encounters with sharks and rays to the serene beauty of the coral reefs. By immersing oneself in the underwater world and embracing the spirit of exploration, travelers can create lasting memories and a deeper appreciation for the islands' extraordinary marine environments.

5.3 Whale Watching and Marine Life

The waters surrounding Tahiti and French Polynesia are a sanctuary for some of the most magnificent marine creatures on the planet. Whale watching and observing marine life in this region offer an unparalleled experience, allowing visitors to witness the awe-inspiring beauty and diversity of the ocean's inhabitants. From the majestic humpback whales to playful dolphins and vibrant coral reefs, the marine life here is nothing short of extraordinary.

Every year, from July to November, humpback whales migrate to the warm waters of French Polynesia to mate and give birth. These gentle giants travel thousands of miles from the icy waters of Antarctica, seeking the tranquil lagoons and sheltered bays of the islands. The island of Rurutu, part of the Austral Islands, is one of the best places to observe these magnificent creatures. The clear, shallow waters provide an ideal setting for whale watching, allowing visitors to see the whales up close as they breach, slap their tails, and perform acrobatic displays. The sight of a humpback whale launching itself out of the water, only to crash back down with a thunderous splash, is a spectacle that leaves a lasting impression.

For those seeking a more immersive experience, swimming with humpback whales is an option in certain areas. Guided tours offer the chance to enter the water and observe these gentle giants in their natural habitat. The experience of being in the presence of such massive creatures, hearing their haunting songs, and witnessing their graceful movements is both humbling and exhilarating. It's important to choose responsible tour operators who prioritize the well-being of the whales and adhere to strict guidelines to ensure minimal disturbance to these magnificent animals.

Dolphins are another highlight of the marine life in French Polynesia. The island of Moorea is renowned for its resident population of spinner dolphins. These playful and acrobatic creatures are often seen leaping and spinning out of the water, much to the delight of onlookers. Boat tours around Moorea's lagoon offer the chance to observe these dolphins in their natural environment. The clear waters and calm conditions make it easy to spot the dolphins as they swim alongside the boat, often riding the bow wave and putting on a show with their impressive aerial displays.

The island of Tahiti also offers excellent opportunities for dolphin watching. The waters off the coast of Punaauia are home to a population of bottlenose dolphins. These intelligent and social animals are known for their friendly nature and often approach boats out of curiosity. Observing a pod of bottlenose dolphins as they interact with each other, communicate through clicks and whistles, and display their agility is a truly captivating experience.

Beyond the larger marine mammals, the coral reefs of French Polynesia are teeming with life. The vibrant coral gardens are home to a diverse array of fish, invertebrates, and other marine creatures. Snorkeling and diving in these reefs offer a chance to witness the intricate and colorful world beneath the waves. The island of Bora Bora, with its crystal-clear lagoon, is a prime location for exploring coral reefs. The Coral Gardens, located near the eastern coast of the island, are a popular snorkeling spot known for their stunning coral formations and abundant marine life. The shallow waters make it accessible for beginners, while the diverse array of fish, including parrotfish, butterflyfish, and clownfish, ensures a captivating experience for all.

The island of Fakarava, part of the Tuamotu Archipelago, is a UNESCO Biosphere Reserve known for its pristine coral reefs and rich marine biodiversity. The Garuae Pass, the largest pass in French Polynesia, is a renowned diving spot that attracts divers from around the world. The strong currents in the pass create a dynamic underwater environment, teeming with sharks, rays, and schools of fish. The drift dive through Garuae Pass is an exhilarating experience, offering the chance to see a variety of marine life up close. For snorkelers, the shallow areas of the lagoon provide a tranquil and picturesque setting to observe coral gardens and tropical fish.

Sea turtles are another fascinating aspect of French Polynesia's marine life. The islands' lagoons and reefs provide important nesting and feeding grounds for several species of sea turtles, including the green turtle and the hawksbill turtle. The island of Tikehau, with its pink sand beaches and turquoise waters, is a top destination for observing sea turtles. The calm and clear waters of the lagoon make it easy to spot these gentle creatures as they glide gracefully through the water or rest on the sandy seabed. For those interested in conservation, several organizations in French Polynesia are dedicated to protecting sea turtles and their habitats. Participating in a turtle conservation program or visiting a turtle sanctuary can provide a deeper understanding of these remarkable animals and the efforts being made to ensure their survival.

The marine life of French Polynesia is not limited to the larger and more charismatic species. The reefs and lagoons are also home to a myriad of smaller creatures, each playing a vital role in the ecosystem. From the tiny, colorful nudibranchs to the elusive octopuses and the industrious cleaner shrimp, the diversity of marine life is astounding. Exploring the reefs with a keen eye can reveal a hidden world of fascinating and often overlooked creatures.

Engaging in whale watching and observing marine life in Tahiti and French Polynesia offers a unique opportunity to connect with the natural world and gain a deeper appreciation for the ocean's inhabitants. Whether witnessing the awe-inspiring breaching of humpback whales, swimming with playful dolphins, or exploring the vibrant coral reefs, the experiences are both educational and inspiring. The rich marine biodiversity of the region highlights the importance of conservation efforts to protect these fragile ecosystems and ensure that future generations can continue to enjoy the wonders of the underwater world. By embracing responsible tourism practices and supporting conservation initiatives, visitors can contribute to the preservation of French Polynesia's extraordinary marine life and create lasting memories of their encounters with the ocean's most magnificent creatures.

5.4 Water Sports and Activities

The allure of Tahiti and French Polynesia extends far beyond its idyllic beaches and stunning landscapes. The islands offer a plethora of water sports and activities that cater to both adrenaline junkies and those seeking a more leisurely experience. The warm, crystal-clear waters and consistent trade winds create the perfect environment for a wide range of aquatic adventures, making it a paradise for water enthusiasts.

Surfing is one of the most popular water sports in Tahiti, attracting surfers from around the globe. The island is home to some of the world's most famous surf breaks, including Teahupo'o, renowned for its massive, barreling waves. This legendary wave is not for the faint-hearted and is best suited for experienced surfers. However, there are plenty of other surf spots around the islands that cater to all skill levels. The island of Moorea, for example, offers more accessible waves that are perfect for beginners. Surf schools and rental shops are readily available, providing lessons and equipment for those looking to catch their first wave.

Kitesurfing and windsurfing are also immensely popular in French Polynesia, thanks to the consistent trade winds and expansive lagoons. The island of Bora Bora, with its shallow, turquoise waters and steady winds, is a top destination for both sports. The lagoon provides a safe and picturesque setting for kitesurfers and windsurfers to glide across the water, performing jumps and tricks. For those new to the sport, several schools offer lessons and equipment rental, ensuring a safe and enjoyable experience.

For a more tranquil water activity, stand-up paddleboarding (SUP) offers a unique way to explore the islands' lagoons and coastline. The calm, clear waters make it easy to paddle at a leisurely pace, taking in the stunning scenery and observing marine life below. Paddleboarding around the island of Huahine, for example, allows visitors to explore hidden coves, mangroves, and coral gardens. The gentle exercise and peaceful surroundings make SUP a perfect activity for all ages and fitness levels.

Snorkeling is another must-do activity in French Polynesia, given the vibrant coral reefs and abundant marine life. The island of Rangiroa, part of the Tuamotu Archipelago, is renowned for its exceptional snorkeling opportunities. The Blue Lagoon, a secluded area within the atoll, offers crystal-clear waters and an array of colorful fish, rays, and even small sharks. Snorkeling here feels like swimming in an aquarium, with the added thrill of encountering larger marine creatures. Equipment rental is widely available, and guided tours can provide additional insights into the underwater world.

For those seeking a more immersive experience, scuba diving in French Polynesia is unparalleled. The islands boast some of the best dive sites in the world, with diverse marine life and stunning underwater landscapes. The island of Fakarava, a UNESCO Biosphere Reserve, is a prime diving destination. The Garuae Pass, the largest pass in French Polynesia, offers thrilling drift dives where divers can encounter sharks, rays, and schools of fish. The South Pass, known for its coral walls and vibrant marine life, is another highlight. Dive operators in the region offer courses for beginners, as well as guided dives for certified divers, ensuring a safe and unforgettable experience.

Sailing is another fantastic way to explore the islands and their surrounding waters. Chartering a sailboat or catamaran allows visitors to navigate the lagoons and visit remote islands and motus (small islets). The Society Islands, including Tahiti, Moorea, and Bora Bora, are particularly popular for sailing, with their sheltered lagoons and stunning anchorages. Sailing provides the freedom to explore at one's own pace, discovering hidden beaches, snorkeling spots, and picturesque villages. Many charter companies offer crewed or bareboat options, catering to both experienced sailors and those new to the sport.

Kayaking is a wonderful way to explore the lagoons and coastline of French Polynesia at a leisurely pace. The calm waters and stunning scenery make it an ideal activity for all ages. Kayaking around the island of Taha'a, known as the "Vanilla Island," offers the chance to paddle through tranquil lagoons, visit pearl farms, and explore lush, tropical landscapes. The island's serene environment and gentle waters make it a perfect destination for a relaxing kayaking adventure.

Fishing enthusiasts will find plenty of opportunities to indulge in their passion in French Polynesia. The islands' rich marine life and diverse fishing grounds make it a prime destination for both deep-sea and lagoon fishing. The waters around the island of Raiatea, for example, are known for their abundance of game fish, including marlin, tuna, and mahi-mahi. Local fishing charters offer guided trips, providing all the necessary equipment and expertise to ensure a successful and enjoyable fishing experience.

For a truly unique water activity, visitors can try their hand at traditional Polynesian outrigger canoeing. The va'a, or outrigger canoe, is an integral part of Polynesian culture and history. Paddling a va'a offers a glimpse into the traditional way of life and provides a deeper connection to the islands' heritage. Several operators offer guided outrigger canoe tours, allowing visitors to learn the techniques and experience the thrill of paddling through the lagoons and along the coastline.

Jet skiing is another exciting way to explore the waters of French Polynesia. The island of Bora Bora, with its expansive lagoon and stunning scenery, is a popular destination for jet skiing. Guided tours take visitors around the island, stopping at key points of interest and providing opportunities for snorkeling and swimming. The thrill of speeding across the turquoise waters, combined with the breathtaking views, makes jet skiing an exhilarating adventure.

For those looking to relax and unwind, a leisurely boat cruise offers a perfect way to take in the beauty of the islands. Sunset cruises around the island of Moorea, for example, provide a romantic and serene experience. As the sun sets over the horizon, casting a golden glow over the water, guests can enjoy a glass of champagne and the tranquil ambiance. Many cruises also include opportunities for snorkeling, swimming, and even dolphin watching, adding to the overall experience.

The diverse range of water sports and activities in Tahiti and French Polynesia ensures that there is something for everyone, whether seeking adventure or relaxation. The islands' natural beauty, combined with the warm, inviting waters, create an unparalleled setting for aquatic adventures. By embracing the opportunities to explore the lagoons, reefs, and coastline, visitors can create lasting memories and gain a deeper appreciation for the unique and vibrant marine environment of French Polynesia.

CHAPTER 6: RELAXATION AND LUXURY

6.1 Overwater Bungalows and Resorts

Imagine waking up to the gentle lapping of waves beneath your feet, the sun casting a golden glow over the turquoise waters, and the scent of tropical flowers wafting through the air. This is the quintessential experience of staying in an overwater bungalow in Tahiti and French Polynesia. These luxurious accommodations, perched on stilts above the lagoon, offer an unparalleled blend of comfort, privacy, and breathtaking natural beauty.

The concept of overwater bungalows originated in French Polynesia in the 1960s, and since then, they have become synonymous with luxury travel in the region. These bungalows are designed to provide guests with direct access to the lagoon, allowing for activities such as snorkeling, swimming, and kayaking right from their private decks. The crystal-clear waters teem with vibrant marine life, making every dip an adventure.

One of the most iconic destinations for overwater bungalows is Bora Bora. Known as the "Pearl of the Pacific," Bora Bora boasts some of the most luxurious resorts in the world. The Four Seasons Resort Bora Bora, for instance, offers spacious overwater bungalows with glass floor panels, allowing guests to observe the underwater world from the comfort of their living room. Each bungalow is elegantly furnished, featuring traditional Polynesian decor with modern amenities. The resort also offers a range of activities, from guided snorkeling tours to sunset cruises, ensuring that guests can make the most of their stay.

Another renowned resort in Bora Bora is the St. Regis Bora Bora Resort. This resort takes luxury to the next level with its overwater villas, each equipped with a private plunge pool and butler service. The villas are designed to provide maximum privacy, with expansive decks offering panoramic views of Mount Otemanu and the surrounding lagoon. The resort's Lagoon Restaurant, helmed by renowned chef Jean-Georges Vongerichten, offers a culinary experience that complements the stunning natural setting.

Moorea, just a short ferry ride from Tahiti, is another prime destination for overwater bungalows. The Hilton Moorea Lagoon Resort & Spa offers a range of overwater bungalows, each with direct access to the lagoon. The resort's bungalows feature contemporary Polynesian design, with thatched roofs, wooden floors, and large windows that frame the stunning views. Guests can enjoy a variety of activities, from paddleboarding to exploring the island's lush interior on a guided tour.

For those seeking a more intimate and secluded experience, the island of Taha'a offers the perfect escape. The Le Taha'a Island Resort & Spa, located on a private islet, offers overwater suites that blend seamlessly with the natural surroundings. Each suite features a spacious deck with direct access to the lagoon, as well as an outdoor shower and a hammock for ultimate relaxation. The resort's spa, set amidst a tropical garden, offers a range of treatments inspired by traditional Polynesian techniques, providing a holistic approach to relaxation and rejuvenation.

Rangiroa, one of the largest atolls in the world, offers a unique overwater bungalow experience at the Hotel Kia Ora Resort & Spa. The resort's overwater bungalows are designed to provide guests with uninterrupted views of the lagoon and the open ocean beyond. Each bungalow features a private deck with a ladder leading directly into the water, allowing for easy access to the vibrant coral reefs that surround the atoll. The resort also offers a range of activities, from diving excursions to dolphin watching tours, ensuring that guests can fully immerse themselves in the natural beauty of Rangiroa.

The island of Huahine, known for its lush landscapes and rich cultural heritage, offers a more laid-back and authentic overwater bungalow experience. The Royal Huahine Resort, located on a secluded beach, offers overwater bungalows that provide a perfect blend of comfort and simplicity. Each bungalow features a private deck with direct access to the lagoon, as well as a glass floor panel for observing the marine life below. The resort's restaurant, set on a terrace overlooking the lagoon, offers a menu of fresh, locally-sourced ingredients, providing a true taste of Polynesian cuisine.

For those seeking the ultimate in luxury and exclusivity, The Brando on the private island of Tetiaroa offers an unparalleled experience. While not strictly overwater bungalows, the resort's beachfront villas offer direct access to the lagoon and are designed to provide the utmost in privacy and comfort. Each villa features a private plunge pool, an outdoor bathtub, and a spacious deck with stunning views of the lagoon. The resort's commitment to sustainability and conservation is evident in every aspect of its design and operation, making it a perfect choice for eco-conscious travelers.

The allure of overwater bungalows in Tahiti and French Polynesia lies not only in their luxurious amenities but also in their ability to provide a unique and immersive experience of the natural beauty of the region. The combination of stunning landscapes, vibrant marine life, and the warm hospitality of the Polynesian people creates an unforgettable experience that lingers long after the journey ends.

When planning a stay in an overwater bungalow, it's important to consider the time of year and the specific location. The dry season, from May to October, offers the best weather for outdoor activities and exploring the lagoon. However, the shoulder seasons of April and November can also be a great time to visit, with fewer crowds and more availability at the resorts.

It's also worth considering the range of activities and amenities offered by each resort. While some resorts focus on providing a tranquil and relaxing experience, others offer a wide range of activities, from water sports to cultural tours. Whether you're seeking adventure or relaxation, there's an overwater bungalow experience in Tahiti and French Polynesia to suit your preferences.

In conclusion, the overwater bungalows and resorts of Tahiti and French Polynesia offer a unique and luxurious way to experience the natural beauty of the region. From the iconic bungalows of Bora Bora to the secluded retreats of Taha'a and Rangiroa, each destination offers its own unique charm and allure. Whether you're celebrating a special occasion or simply seeking a tranquil escape, the overwater bungalows of Tahiti and French Polynesia provide an unforgettable experience that will leave you longing to return.

6.2 Spa and Wellness Retreats

The allure of Tahiti and French Polynesia extends beyond its stunning landscapes and crystal-clear waters. For those seeking relaxation and rejuvenation, the region offers an array of world-class spa and wellness retreats that promise to soothe the mind, body, and soul. These sanctuaries of serenity are nestled in some of the most picturesque locations, providing an idyllic backdrop for a transformative wellness experience.

One of the most renowned spa destinations in French Polynesia is the InterContinental Bora Bora Resort & Thalasso Spa. This luxurious resort is home to the Deep Ocean Spa, which is the first thalassotherapy center in the South Pacific. Thalassotherapy, a treatment that uses seawater and marine products for therapeutic purposes, is at the heart of the spa's offerings. Guests can indulge in a variety of treatments, including hydrotherapy baths, seaweed wraps, and marine-based facials. The spa's overwater treatment rooms provide a unique setting, allowing guests to gaze at the vibrant marine life below as they unwind.

On the island of Moorea, the Sofitel Moorea Ia Ora Beach Resort offers a tranquil spa experience at the Le Jardin Spa & Beauty. This spa is set amidst lush tropical gardens, creating a serene environment that enhances the relaxation process. The spa's treatments are inspired by traditional Polynesian techniques and use locally-sourced ingredients such as coconut oil, vanilla, and tamanu oil. Guests can choose from a range of massages, body scrubs, and facials, each designed to promote relaxation and rejuvenation. The spa also offers couples' treatments, making it a perfect choice for honeymooners or those celebrating a special occasion.

Taha'a, known as the "Vanilla Island," is home to the Le Taha'a Island Resort & Spa, which offers a unique wellness experience at the Manea Spa. The spa is nestled in a lush garden, surrounded by the island's famous vanilla plantations. The treatments at Manea Spa are inspired by Polynesian traditions and incorporate the island's natural resources. Guests can enjoy a variety of massages, body treatments, and facials, all designed to promote relaxation and well-being. The spa's signature treatment, the Taurumi massage, is a traditional Polynesian massage that uses rhythmic movements and natural oils to release tension and restore balance.

For those seeking a more holistic wellness experience, The Brando on the private island of Tetiaroa offers an unparalleled retreat. The Varua Te Ora Polynesian Spa at The Brando is a haven of tranquility, set amidst a lush tropical forest. The spa's treatments are inspired by ancient Polynesian traditions and use natural ingredients sourced from the island. Guests can choose from a range of massages, body treatments, and facials, each designed to promote relaxation and rejuvenation. The spa also offers yoga and meditation sessions, providing a holistic approach to wellness. The Brando's commitment to sustainability and conservation is evident in every aspect of the spa, making it a perfect choice for eco-conscious travelers.

Rangiroa, one of the largest atolls in the world, offers a unique spa experience at the Hotel Kia Ora Resort & Spa. The resort's Poekura Spa is set amidst a tropical garden, providing a serene environment for relaxation. The spa's treatments are inspired by traditional Polynesian techniques and use locally-sourced ingredients such as coconut oil and vanilla. Guests can enjoy a variety of massages, body treatments, and facials, each designed to promote relaxation and well-being. The spa also offers couples' treatments, making it a perfect choice for honeymooners or those celebrating a special occasion.

On the island of Huahine, the Royal Huahine Resort offers a tranquil spa experience at the Manea Spa. The spa is set amidst lush tropical gardens, creating a serene environment that enhances the relaxation process. The spa's treatments are inspired by traditional Polynesian techniques and use locally-sourced ingredients such as coconut oil, vanilla, and tamanu oil. Guests can choose from a range of massages, body scrubs, and facials, each designed to promote relaxation and rejuvenation. The spa also offers couples' treatments, making it a perfect choice for honeymooners or those celebrating a special occasion.

The island of Tahiti itself is home to several luxurious spa and wellness retreats. The InterContinental Tahiti Resort & Spa offers a tranquil spa experience at the Deep Nature Spa. The spa is set amidst lush tropical gardens, providing a serene environment for relaxation. The spa's treatments are inspired by traditional Polynesian techniques and use locally-sourced ingredients such as coconut oil, vanilla, and tamanu oil. Guests can choose from a range of massages, body scrubs, and facials, each designed to promote relaxation and rejuvenation. The spa also offers couples' treatments, making it a perfect choice for honeymooners or those celebrating a special occasion.

For those seeking a more intimate and secluded spa experience, the island of Tikehau offers the perfect escape. The Tikehau Pearl Beach Resort offers a tranquil spa experience at the Tavai Spa. The spa is set amidst lush tropical gardens, creating a serene environment that enhances the relaxation process. The spa's treatments are inspired by traditional Polynesian techniques and use locally-sourced ingredients such as coconut oil, vanilla, and tamanu oil. Guests can choose from a range of massages, body scrubs, and facials, each designed to promote relaxation and rejuvenation. The spa also offers couples' treatments, making it a perfect choice for honeymooners or those celebrating a special occasion.

The allure of spa and wellness retreats in Tahiti and French Polynesia lies not only in their luxurious amenities but also in their ability to provide a unique and immersive experience of the natural beauty of the region. The combination of stunning landscapes, vibrant marine life, and the warm hospitality of the Polynesian people creates an unforgettable experience that lingers long after the journey ends.

When planning a spa and wellness retreat in Tahiti and French Polynesia, it's important to consider the time of year and the specific location. The dry season, from May to October, offers the best weather for outdoor activities and exploring the lagoon.

However, the shoulder seasons of April and November can also be a great time to visit, with fewer crowds and more availability at the resorts.

It's also worth considering the range of activities and amenities offered by each resort. While some resorts focus on providing a tranquil and relaxing experience, others offer a wide range of activities, from water sports to cultural tours. Whether you're seeking adventure or relaxation, there's a spa and wellness retreat in Tahiti and French Polynesia to suit your preferences.

The spa and wellness retreats of Tahiti and French Polynesia offer a unique and luxurious way to experience the natural beauty of the region. From the iconic spas of Bora Bora to the secluded retreats of Taha'a and Rangiroa, each destination offers its own unique charm and allure. Whether you're celebrating a special occasion or simply seeking a tranquil escape, the spa and wellness retreats of Tahiti and French Polynesia provide an unforgettable experience that will leave you longing to return.

6.3 Secluded Beaches

The allure of Tahiti and French Polynesia is not just in its vibrant culture and luxurious resorts but also in its secluded beaches that offer an unparalleled sense of tranquility and privacy. These hidden gems are perfect for those seeking a peaceful retreat away from the bustling tourist spots. The pristine sands, crystal-clear waters, and lush surroundings create an idyllic setting for relaxation and rejuvenation.

One of the most enchanting secluded beaches in French Polynesia is found on the island of Taha'a. Known as the "Vanilla Island," Taha'a is surrounded by a stunning lagoon and offers several hidden beaches that are perfect for a quiet escape. One such beach is located near the Le Taha'a Island Resort & Spa. Accessible only by boat, this beach is a haven of peace and serenity. The soft white sands and turquoise waters are framed by swaying palm trees, creating a picture-perfect setting. Visitors can spend their days lounging on the beach, snorkeling in the clear waters, or simply soaking in the natural beauty of the surroundings.

On the island of Huahine, the secluded beach of Hana Iti offers a tranquil escape from the outside world. This hidden gem is accessible only by boat or a challenging hike, ensuring that it remains a peaceful retreat for those who make the journey. The beach is surrounded by lush vegetation and offers stunning views of the lagoon. The calm waters are perfect for swimming and snorkeling, and the beach itself is ideal for sunbathing or enjoying a picnic. The sense of seclusion and the untouched beauty of Hana Iti make it a must-visit for those seeking a quiet and serene beach experience.

Rangiroa, one of the largest atolls in the world, is home to several secluded beaches that offer a unique and tranquil escape. One such beach is located on the motu (islet) of Tikehau. This remote beach is accessible only by boat and offers a sense of isolation that is perfect for those seeking a peaceful retreat. The pink sands and clear waters create a stunning contrast, and the surrounding coral reefs are teeming with marine life. Visitors can spend their days exploring the underwater world, lounging on the beach, or simply enjoying the natural beauty of the surroundings.

On the island of Moorea, the secluded beach of Temae offers a tranquil escape from the more popular tourist spots. This hidden gem is located on the eastern side of the island and is accessible by a short hike through lush vegetation. The beach is framed by swaying palm trees and offers stunning views of the lagoon and the neighboring island of Tahiti. The calm waters are perfect for swimming and snorkeling, and the beach itself is ideal for sunbathing or enjoying a picnic. The sense of seclusion and the natural beauty of Temae make it a perfect choice for those seeking a quiet and serene beach experience.

The island of Bora Bora, known for its luxurious resorts and stunning overwater bungalows, also offers several secluded beaches that provide a peaceful retreat. One such beach is located on the motu of Tapu. This remote beach is accessible only by boat and offers a sense of isolation that is perfect for those seeking a tranquil escape. The soft white sands and clear waters create a stunning contrast, and the surrounding coral reefs are teeming with marine life. Visitors can spend their days exploring the underwater world, lounging on the beach, or simply enjoying the natural beauty of the surroundings.

On the island of Tahiti, the secluded beach of Plage de Maui offers a tranquil escape from the bustling capital of Papeete. This hidden gem is located on the southern coast of the island and is accessible by a short drive from the city. The beach is framed by swaying palm trees and offers stunning views of the lagoon and the surrounding mountains. The calm waters are perfect for swimming and snorkeling, and the beach itself is ideal for sunbathing or enjoying a picnic. The sense of seclusion and the natural beauty of Plage de Maui make it a perfect choice for those seeking a quiet and serene beach experience.

The island of Tikehau, known for its pink sand beaches and vibrant marine life, offers several secluded beaches that provide a peaceful retreat. One such beach is located on the motu of Tuherahera. This remote beach is accessible only by boat and offers a sense of isolation that is perfect for those seeking a tranquil escape. The pink sands and clear waters create a stunning contrast, and the surrounding coral reefs are teeming with marine life. Visitors can spend their days exploring the underwater world, lounging on the beach, or simply enjoying the natural beauty of the surroundings.

For those seeking a more intimate and secluded beach experience, the island of Fakarava offers the perfect escape. The secluded beach of Tetamanu is located on the southern tip of the island and is accessible only by boat. The beach is framed by swaying palm trees and offers stunning views of the lagoon and the surrounding coral reefs. The calm waters are perfect for swimming and snorkeling, and the beach itself is ideal for sunbathing or enjoying a picnic. The sense of seclusion and the natural beauty of Tetamanu make it a perfect choice for those seeking a quiet and serene beach experience.

The allure of secluded beaches in Tahiti and French Polynesia lies not only in their pristine beauty but also in their ability to provide a unique and immersive experience of the natural surroundings. The combination of stunning landscapes, vibrant marine life, and the warm hospitality of the Polynesian people creates an unforgettable experience that lingers long after the journey ends.

When planning a visit to these secluded beaches, it's important to consider the time of year and the specific location. The dry season, from May to October, offers the best weather for outdoor activities and exploring the lagoon. However, the shoulder seasons of April and November can also be a great time to visit, with fewer crowds and more availability at the resorts.

It's also worth considering the range of activities and amenities offered by each location. While some beaches focus on providing a tranquil and relaxing experience, others offer a wide range of activities, from water sports to cultural tours. Whether you're seeking adventure or relaxation, there's a secluded beach in Tahiti and French Polynesia to suit your preferences.

The secluded beaches of Tahiti and French Polynesia offer a unique and luxurious way to experience the natural beauty of the region. From the iconic beaches of Bora Bora to the hidden gems of Taha'a and Rangiroa, each destination offers its own unique charm and allure. Whether you're celebrating a special occasion or simply seeking a tranquil escape, the secluded beaches of Tahiti and French Polynesia provide an unforgettable experience that will leave you longing to return.

6.4 Romantic Getaways

The islands of Tahiti and French Polynesia have long been synonymous with romance, offering an idyllic backdrop for couples seeking an unforgettable getaway. The combination of stunning natural beauty, luxurious accommodations, and intimate experiences makes this destination perfect for romantic escapes. Whether celebrating a honeymoon, anniversary, or simply the joy of being together, the islands provide a myriad of options to create lasting memories.

Imagine waking up in an overwater bungalow, the gentle sound of waves lapping beneath you, and the first rays of sunlight casting a golden glow over the lagoon. Bora Bora, often referred to as the "Pearl of the Pacific," is renowned for its luxurious overwater bungalows that offer unparalleled privacy and breathtaking views. Resorts like the Four Seasons Bora Bora and the St. Regis Bora Bora Resort provide world-class amenities, including private plunge pools, direct lagoon access, and personalized butler service. Couples can enjoy breakfast delivered by canoe, a private dinner on the beach, or a sunset cruise on a traditional outrigger canoe.

For those seeking a more secluded and intimate experience, the island of Taha'a offers a romantic escape like no other. Known as the "Vanilla Island," Taha'a is surrounded by a stunning lagoon and offers several luxurious resorts that cater to couples. Le Taha'a Island Resort & Spa, located on its own private motu, provides an exclusive and serene setting. The resort's overwater suites and beach villas offer stunning views of the lagoon and the neighboring island of Bora Bora. Couples can indulge in a couples' massage at the resort's spa, enjoy a private picnic on a secluded beach, or take a romantic sunset sail around the island.

Huahine, often referred to as the "Garden Island," offers a more laid-back and authentic Polynesian experience. The island's lush landscapes, pristine beaches, and vibrant culture create a perfect setting for a romantic getaway. The Royal Huahine Resort, accessible only by boat, offers beachfront bungalows and overwater villas that provide a sense of seclusion and tranquility. Couples can explore the island's ancient marae (temples), take a leisurely bike ride through the lush countryside, or enjoy a romantic dinner under the stars at the resort's beachfront restaurant.

Moorea, with its dramatic mountain peaks and crystal-clear lagoons, is another popular destination for couples seeking romance. The island's luxurious resorts, such as the Sofitel Moorea Ia Ora Beach Resort and the Hilton Moorea Lagoon Resort & Spa, offer stunning overwater bungalows and beachfront villas. Couples can enjoy a range of romantic activities, from a private lagoon tour to a couples' spa treatment. The island's lush interior also offers opportunities for adventure, such as hiking to the Belvedere Lookout for panoramic views or taking a 4x4 tour through the island's pineapple plantations.

For a truly unique and unforgettable romantic experience, consider a private yacht charter in the Tuamotu Archipelago. The remote atolls of Rangiroa, Tikehau, and Fakarava offer pristine beaches, vibrant coral reefs, and a sense of isolation that is perfect for a romantic escape. A private yacht charter allows couples to explore these remote islands at their own pace, with the freedom to anchor in secluded lagoons, snorkel in crystal-clear waters, and enjoy gourmet meals prepared by a private chef. The sense of adventure and the stunning natural beauty of the Tuamotus create a perfect setting for romance.

The island of Tahiti, the largest in French Polynesia, also offers several romantic experiences for couples. The InterContinental Tahiti Resort & Spa, located just a short drive from the capital city of Papeete, offers luxurious overwater bungalows and beachfront villas. Couples can enjoy a romantic dinner at the resort's overwater restaurant, Le Lotus, which offers stunning views of the lagoon and the island of Moorea. The resort's spa also offers a range of couples' treatments, including a traditional Polynesian massage and a private jacuzzi overlooking the lagoon.

For those seeking a more adventurous romantic getaway, the island of Nuku Hiva in the Marquesas Islands offers a unique and rugged experience. The island's dramatic landscapes, including towering cliffs, lush valleys, and pristine beaches, create a stunning backdrop for romance. The Keikahanui Nuku Hiva Pearl Lodge offers luxurious bungalows with breathtaking views of the bay and the surrounding mountains. Couples can explore the island's ancient archaeological sites, take a horseback ride through the lush valleys, or enjoy a romantic picnic on a secluded beach.

The islands of Tahiti and French Polynesia also offer several unique cultural experiences that can add a special touch to a romantic getaway. Couples can participate in a traditional Polynesian wedding ceremony, complete with flower crowns, traditional music, and a blessing by a Tahitian priest. Many resorts offer wedding packages that include everything from the ceremony to a romantic dinner on the beach. For those celebrating an anniversary or renewing their vows, a traditional Polynesian ceremony can create a memorable and meaningful experience.

The vibrant marine life of French Polynesia also offers several unique and romantic experiences for couples. Snorkeling or diving in the crystal-clear waters of the lagoon provides an opportunity to explore the vibrant coral reefs and swim with colorful fish, rays, and even sharks. Many resorts offer private snorkeling or diving tours, allowing couples to explore the underwater world at their own pace. For a truly unforgettable experience, consider a private manta ray or dolphin encounter, where couples can swim with these gentle creatures in their natural habitat.

The islands of Tahiti and French Polynesia offer a perfect blend of luxury, natural beauty, and unique experiences that create an ideal setting for romance. Whether lounging in an overwater bungalow, exploring a secluded beach, or enjoying a private yacht charter, couples can create lasting memories in this stunning paradise. The warm hospitality of the Polynesian people, combined with the breathtaking landscapes and luxurious accommodations, ensures that a romantic getaway in Tahiti and French Polynesia will be an unforgettable experience.

6.5 Sunset Cruises

The allure of a sunset cruise in Tahiti and French Polynesia is undeniable. As the sun dips below the horizon, painting the sky with hues of orange, pink, and purple, the tranquil waters of the South Pacific provide the perfect setting for an unforgettable experience. Whether aboard a luxurious catamaran, a traditional Polynesian outrigger canoe, or a private yacht, a sunset cruise offers a unique way to soak in the natural beauty and serenity of these islands.

Imagine stepping onto a sleek catamaran, greeted by a friendly crew and the gentle sway of the boat. As you set sail, the warm tropical breeze caresses your skin, and the rhythmic sound of the waves creates a soothing soundtrack. The islands of Bora Bora, Moorea, and Tahiti offer some of the most picturesque settings for a sunset cruise. In Bora Bora, the iconic Mount Otemanu serves as a dramatic backdrop, while the crystal-clear lagoon reflects the changing colors of the sky. The Four Seasons Bora Bora and the Conrad Bora Bora Nui are among the resorts that offer private sunset cruises, complete with champagne and gourmet canapés.

For a more intimate and authentic experience, consider a sunset cruise on a traditional Polynesian outrigger canoe. These canoes, known as va'a, have been used by the Polynesians for centuries and offer a unique way to connect with the local culture. In Moorea, the Moorea Beach Lodge offers sunset cruises on their traditional outrigger canoe, allowing guests to experience the island's stunning coastline and vibrant marine life. As the sun sets, the crew often shares stories and legends of the islands, adding a cultural dimension to the experience.

Private yacht charters provide the ultimate in luxury and exclusivity for a sunset cruise. The Tuamotu Archipelago, with its remote atolls and pristine waters, offers a perfect setting for a private yacht experience. Companies like Tahiti Yacht Charter and Dream Yacht Charter offer a range of options, from intimate sailboats to luxurious catamarans. A private yacht charter allows you to explore the remote atolls of Rangiroa, Tikehau, and Fakarava at your own pace, anchoring in secluded lagoons and enjoying the sunset in complete privacy. The crew can prepare a gourmet dinner on board, featuring fresh local seafood and tropical fruits, creating a truly unforgettable dining experience.

The island of Tahiti, the largest in French Polynesia, also offers several options for sunset cruises. The InterContinental Tahiti Resort & Spa, located near the capital city of Papeete, offers sunset cruises on their luxurious catamaran. Guests can enjoy stunning views of the island's rugged coastline and the neighboring island of Moorea. The resort's sunset cruise includes a selection of canapés and cocktails, allowing guests to relax and unwind as they watch the sun set over the Pacific Ocean.

For those seeking a more adventurous sunset cruise, the island of Huahine offers a unique and off-the-beaten-path experience.

Known as the "Garden Island," Huahine's lush landscapes and pristine beaches create a stunning backdrop for a sunset cruise. The Royal Huahine Resort offers sunset cruises on their traditional outrigger canoe, allowing guests to explore the island's coastline and vibrant coral reefs. As the sun sets, the crew often plays traditional Polynesian music, creating a magical and unforgettable atmosphere.

The Marquesas Islands, with their dramatic landscapes and rich cultural heritage, offer a unique setting for a sunset cruise. The island of Nuku Hiva, with its towering cliffs and lush valleys, provides a stunning backdrop for a sunset sail. The Keikahanui Nuku Hiva Pearl Lodge offers sunset cruises on their traditional outrigger canoe, allowing guests to experience the island's rugged beauty and vibrant marine life. As the sun sets, the crew often shares stories and legends of the Marquesas, adding a cultural dimension to the experience.

The vibrant marine life of French Polynesia also adds a unique element to a sunset cruise. The islands' crystal-clear waters are home to a diverse array of marine species, including colorful fish, rays, and even dolphins. Many sunset cruises include opportunities for snorkeling or diving, allowing guests to explore the underwater world as the sun sets. In Bora Bora, the Lagoon Service offers sunset cruises that include snorkeling with rays and sharks, providing a thrilling and unforgettable experience.

The islands of Tahiti and French Polynesia also offer several unique cultural experiences that can be incorporated into a sunset cruise. Many resorts and tour operators offer traditional Polynesian music and dance performances on board, creating a festive and authentic atmosphere. Guests can also participate in a traditional Polynesian blessing ceremony, complete with flower crowns and traditional chants. These cultural experiences add a special touch to a sunset cruise, creating lasting memories and a deeper connection to the islands.

The warm hospitality of the Polynesian people, combined with the breathtaking landscapes and luxurious accommodations, ensures that a sunset cruise in Tahiti and French Polynesia will be an unforgettable experience. Whether aboard a luxurious catamaran, a traditional outrigger canoe, or a private yacht, a sunset cruise offers a unique way to soak in the natural beauty and serenity of these islands. The changing colors of the sky, the gentle sway of the boat, and the soothing sound of the waves create a magical and unforgettable atmosphere, making a sunset cruise a must-do experience for any visitor to Tahiti and French Polynesia.

THANK YOU!

As you close the pages of this travel guide, I wish to extend our heartfelt gratitude for choosing to explore the wonders of Tahiti and French Polynesia with us. This journey, though captured in words and images, is but a prelude to the vibrant experiences that await you in this paradise on Earth. Your decision to delve into the hidden gems, cultural treasures, and thrilling adventures of these islands speaks volumes about your spirit of exploration and your desire to connect with the world in a meaningful way.

Tahiti and French Polynesia are not just destinations; they are living, breathing entities that pulse with life, history, and beauty. From the moment you set foot on these islands, you are embraced by the warmth of the Polynesian people, whose smiles and hospitality are as radiant as the sun that kisses the turquoise waters. It is our hope that this guide has not only informed you but also inspired you to immerse yourself fully in the experiences that these islands offer.

BONUS 1: TAHITI FAMILY TRIP IDEA

BONUS 2: TWO WEEKS - TUAMOTO ARCHIPELAGO AND SOCIETY ISLANDS TRIP

BONUS 3: TAHITI TRAVEL PLANNER

Made in the USA
Las Vegas, NV
10 October 2024